"The essays by the writers featured in You've Got This Mama, Too made me feel like I had just made twenty-two new trusted friends, also navigating the identity-warping maze of being a mother, with their honest, intelligent and poignant accounts of motherhood. The best compliment? I stayed up way, way past my bedtime, because I couldn't put this book down."

~ Rebecca Eckler, Executive Editor of SavvyMom and author of Blissfully Blended Bullshit

"Messy and hard, beautiful and tender – motherhood is truly a sanctifying experience. Community with other mamas helps us muddle through, lifts us up and brings so much joy. You've Got This, Mama, Too offers up a collected community of women who share their unique, intimate and inspiring stories. Like sister-friends sharing a cup of coffee, they let us know that no matter where we're at on our motherhood journey, we're not alone. This encouragement enables us to toss perfection to the wind, assures us we can handle today and gives us hope for tomorrow, for we're all still becoming."

~ Natalie Fieleke, Writer at Lifestyle Publications | Blogger | Social Media Manager | Mama x 2 | @lovely.inside.out | @lifestylepublications | @kcmomsblog

"There are incredible life-lessons in every single chapter of this book; whether the story mirrors your own personal experience or not. Then, you'll find your chapter, and experience an immeasurable feeling of connection that's unheard of in the written medium. Oh, and you're definitely going to cry. Like, a lot."

~ Courtney St Croix, Best selling author | Podcast Host - Momfidence Podcast | Women's Confidence Coach | Mama x 1 | www.momfidentaf.com | Ig: @MomfidentAF

"These mamas pour out their hearts - sharing raw, genuine truths about motherhood. You will be encouraged by their stories and gain a connection with each one that will resonate with you long after the final chapter ends."

~ Nicole Hughes, Founder of Levi's Legacy | Survivor of Child Loss | Writer www.levislegacy.com | Ig:@nicolehughes8

"As a woman who doesn't have children, and isn't entirely sure she wants them, I didn't think I'd be able to relate much to the stories in You've Got This Mama, Too when I sat down to edit it. How wrong I was. The authors in this book touch on themes that affect all women, mothers or not - the need to take care of ourselves, the desire to find fulfillment in our days, the drive to nurture and protect the people we love, the ability to be resilient in the face of soul-shattering loss. If I ever become a mother, I will be so much less scared knowing that there is such a tribe of incredible women standing behind me."

~ Sara Gustafson, Best selling author | Editor | Meditation Coach

"You've Got This, Mama, Too raises awareness for the myriad of battles women face daily: fertility, miscarriage, loss, marriage, motherhood, health diagnoses, and more. It felt as though I was not alone: that I have my own tribe in each of these women. They are inspiring and true warriors. Each story makes me want to kick ass at life even more, no matter the setback or cards dealt because these women rock! Mamas rock!"

~ Tania Moraes-Vaz, Best selling author | Editor | Multipreneur | Mama x 1 | www.taniajanemoraesvaz.com

"Struggles and overwhelm. Love and joy. I love how this book shows all different aspects of motherhood, allowing us all to be the mothers we are. No one is perfect and feeling the relief of knowing we are not alone in the trials and tribulations, of not only being a mom to our children, but also owning our own life story. Thank you to all of these amazing women who boldly share their stories, giving us all the courage to appreciate our own."

~ Rhonda Ramsay, BSc in Psychology | Health & Nutrition Coach | Author | Speaker | Business owner | Cancer thriver | Creator of the Pink Project - Helping redefine the way people think, cope, and live with cancer | Mama x 2 | www.pinkproject.net | @rjramsay36

"Reading these heartfelt stories I am reminded of the value of being authentically YOU and ME. With the ups and downs of life, we can all learn so much from sharing our truths and being transparent in our struggles and triumphs. Because at the end of the day it is our humanness that truly connects us all! Thank you so much for the reminder!"

~ Lara Bolton, Professional Keynote Speaker | Owner of The Revenue Pros | Direct Selling Pro | Mama x 2

"The honesty and vulnerability of these mamas is so refreshing. Even though our stories are different, I think it's safe to say we can all relate to the feelings expressed in this book. As moms, it is so important to keep the conversation going so that we don't feel isolated or alone. The moms in this book write about what all moms are thinking but don't say out loud. Thank you for your courage. Together, we've got this mamas."

~ Chelsea Burwash, Owner of Project YOU and West Coast Chic Resale | Mama x1 | @iamprojectyou | @wcchicboutique

"When raising a child we are also raising ourselves as mothers and this book embraces the journey, creating a safe place for all; hopeful mothers to be, expecting moms, and moms at any stage. The raw and heartfelt stories are touching, inspiring and weave us together as a universal community in motherhood with beauty, grace, and love. I wish there had been a book like this when I first became a mom.

~ Deirdre Slattery, BHK, BED | Fitness and Health Consultant and Coach | Published Fitness Model | Author | Single mama x 1 | @Deirdre_sfitness

YOU'VE GOT THIS, *Mama,* TOO

A MOTHER'S GUIDE TO EMBRACING IMPERFECTION
& LIVING AN AUTHENTIC LIFE

YOU'VE GOT THIS, *Mama,* TOO

A MOTHER'S GUIDE TO EMBRACING IMPERFECTION & LIVING AN AUTHENTIC LIFE

SABRINA GREER *featuring The Mama Tribe*

CHARLEYNE OULTON · HABIBA JESSICA ZAMAN · CASSIE JEANS · JESSICA LANCE
JESSICA SHARPE · MEGHAN KRMPOTIC · TIA SLIGHTHAM · LISA MECHOR
JILLIAN WEST · SHERRI MARIE GAUDET · SAMANTHA AMARAEGBU · SHAYLA WEY
BEX BUCCI · SARAH SECOR-MACELROY · CARRIE BRUNO · AIMEE SWIFT
NIA PYCIOR · TAELAR HOWE · JUSTINE DOWD · DANIELLE WILLIAMS · LISA AAMOT

GOLDEN BRICK ROAD
PUBLISHING HOUSE

YOU'VE GOT THIS, MAMA
YGT *Mama*
WWW.YGTMAMA.COM

Published in Canada, for Global Distribution by Golden Brick Road Publishing House Inc.
www.goldenbrickroad.pub

For more information email: sabrina@ygtmama.com

ISBN:
trade paperback: 978-1-988736-58-7
ebook: 978-1-988736-59-4
kindle: 978-1-988736-60-0

To order additional copies of this book: orders@gbrph.ca

CONTENTS

Introduction · 9
by SABRINA GREER

SECTION 1: There's No Such Thing as Perfect Timing · 15
by SABRINA GREER

Lighting My Darkness · 19
by BEX BUCCI

The Magical Thinking Paradox · 33
by SARAH SECOR-MACELROY

Learning to Love Myself · 45
by HABIBA JESSICA ZAMAN

Finding Joy in Unease · 57
by CARRIE BRUNO

The Unconditional · 69
by CASSIE JEANS

SECTION 2: Even Miracles Aren't Perfect · 79
by SABRINA GREER

Joy in the Unexpected · 83
by AIMEE SWIFT

Coming Home · 95
by JESSICA SHARPE

Note to Self: You Made It · 109
by JESSICA LANCE

Anxiety: The Invisible Barrier · 123
by TIA SLIGHTHAM

Cancer Is Not a Choice, Happiness Is · 135
by LISA MECHOR

SECTION 3: Embracing The Imperfect Journey · 147
by SABRINA GREER

There Is Glory in The Gory · 151
by NIA PYCIOR

It's Harder Than You Think · 161
by MEGHAN KRMPOTIC

Lessons in Loss · 173
by TAELAR HOWE

Follow Your Dreams, They Know the Way · 185
by JUSTINE DOWD

Finding Magic in Madness · 199
by DANIELLE WILLIAMS

SECTION 4: Our Imperfect Pasts Do Not Define Us · 213
by SABRINA GREER

Shadow Work · 217
by JILLIAN WEST

Beginning Again · 229
by CHARLEYNE OULTON

Life Happens · 241
by SHERRI MARIE GAUDET

Babies Shouldn't Have Babies · 253
by SAMANTHA AMARAEGBU

My Journey to Becoming A MomBoss · 263
by SHAYLA WEY

Bliss in the Chaos · 277
by LISA AAMOT

Final Thoughts · 289
By SABRINA GREER & ELAINE KALEY

INTRODUCTION

By Sabrina Greer

"We are united; I have found my tribe in the collective voice of the beautiful Mother."

*"Imperfections are not inadequacies; they are reminders
that we're all in this together."*
~ Brené Brown

erfection, as defined by the Merriam-Webster Dictionary, is *the condition, state, or quality of being free or as free as possible from all flaws or defects.* Let that soak in for a moment . . .

Now I'll throw the definition of **a perfectionist** at you: *a person who refuses to accept any standard short of* **perfection**.

Guilty? Me too, Mama! You are not alone.

When we wrote *You've Got This, Mama - A Mother's Guide To Embracing The Chaos & Living An Empowered Life,* I saw a common theme in the stories shared, and I remembered all the questions that came up for me on my personal journey into motherhood.

Was I meant to be a mother? Will I ever be a mother? Will I make a good mother? What if? Why me? How come?

There was always so much chatter and noise in my head. *What are these constant voices that speak up so often?* I've heard them referred to as many things in my research: the Ego, your inner mean girl, evil roommate Susan upstairs, and the devil on your shoulder.

Whatever you call them, they all mean the same thing: that piece of your psyche that wants to fight your greatness and keep you small. The voice that asks all the wrong questions and, in turn, makes you question your very worth.

The voice that tells you, *You need to be perfect, so-and-so is better than you, you aren't good enough, pretty enough, fit enough, worthy enough.*

If you ask me, we all need to tell her to shut the EFF up!

I was one of those mamas who struggled with the first question most of all. *Was I meant to be a mother?* I didn't dream of having children when I was but a child myself. I didn't have a scrapbook filled with wedding dress cutouts or a journal filled with my future children's names. I had dreams, and not one of them involved children. They were dreams of travel, of Hollywood-type romances and wild adventures.

I always assumed that once you had babies, it meant you were old and somehow life was no longer about you. *Don't you become all consumed by this little life you've created?*

I like sleep. I like sex. Correction: I *love* sleep, and I *love* sex. I *love* to travel. I *love* spontaneity! I have goals, ambitions, massive throbbing passions. *Aren't you forced to give up the things you are passionate about once you have children?*

Does this make me selfish? This was another question that continuously crept in, even before the infamous *mom-guilt* showed up. I had immense shame around this. I love kids. I have had several dozen foster siblings. I have a university degree in developmental psychology and early childhood education. *Wasn't I somehow trained to be a mother? Wouldn't I be doing the world a disservice by not reproducing?*

I often joked with my peers that I enjoyed children as long as they came with a twenty-four-hour return policy. This was true for me for a long time. I was thirty-two years old when I had my first biological child. My hubby and I had only been together for one year, but somehow we just knew it was time. I have to believe until that point, my guardian angels had been administering baby repellant until the right partner — my true family — came along. My eldest came to me ready-made at the (what is still to this day my favorite) age of six. It was such an amazing transition. No "You're not my mother" pushback, just tons of love. I will forever cherish this relationship because every day I get to *choose* him as my son.

You'll experience so many different schools of thought as you read the pages of this book. We have an entire section on mamas who maybe didn't always feel cut out to be mamas. We also have an entire section on the exact opposite: the women knew it was their destiny to have children and who have committed a massive portion of their lives and bodies to that destiny. Honestly, we could have compiled an entire book series based on fertility alone and the women who spent new-home-worthy dollars to get one step closer to having a baby. Years of invasive treatments, poking, prodding, hormone therapies, countless disappointments, and living in the shadows of their own lives for years: these women are warriors, living, breathing superheroes.

That's what I love most about these books and exactly why they came to be. They allow our complexities as human beings to shine bright. We are truly united in our differences. Our journeys into motherhood are all so drastically different, but we are here and we are in this together. How we arrived at this point in our journey is not important. There is no right or wrong answer to any of it.

It is okay if one mama stumbled into motherhood by accident and another spent nearly a decade fighting for the same outcome. These are the authentic memoirs of the women who experienced them. I've discovered in my research that I don't need to feel guilty about my story because someone has suffered *more* or *less*, done things *better* or *worse*. Why? Because it's *my* story and *mine* alone; it's all so subjective anyhow. I have found my tribe in the collective voice of the beautiful Mother. What I've realized while reading the hearts and souls that grace these pages is that the *how* doesn't matter. **How** our babies were conceived, **how** our pregnancies played out, whether or not our *perfect* birth plans were followed to a T, or **how** that baby came to be born. **How** they receive nourishment, **how** they learn, develop, grow. What matters is they have found their way home — home to you, Mama. Your precious little gift is right where they're meant to be.

You will also read an entire section on our tiny warriors — in some cases, extra tiny at only two pounds. Mini heroes who came into this world with a bang, and a little extra to overcome. At some point, we've all been told by some well-meaning loved one, or even stranger, "You won't be dealt cards you can't play somehow" or "You won't be handed circumstances you cannot handle." These stories are the tougher hands for sure. Somehow, though, these fierce warrior babes and mamas play them with such grace.

You will hopefully learn that it doesn't matter whether or not you directly relate to each and every voice or experience. You do not need to have a child with debilitating anxiety, cancer, or Down syndrome to be inspired by the strength of these incredible humans (mamas and babes alike).

You see, we all relate. We love our children with such a powerful kind of love that it is tough to explain. It doesn't matter whether you didn't initially *plan for* them or whether you gave up everything you had to find them. It does not matter if they were born with layered challenges or are the picture of health. It does not matter if they were pulled through an incision in your tummy or flew out of your who-who en route to the hospital. What matters is that we stand together and support one another.

Theodore Roosevelt said it best: *"Comparison is the thief of joy."* This quote holds true in all facets of life, but most of all, it holds true in this joyful, heart-wrenching, heart-warming, and crazy adventure called motherhood. How can we possibly *compare* our journeys? Pain is pain. Grief is grief. Love is love. Joy is joy. How can we say one person's emotions are more authentic or important than another's? What gives us that right?

This book was carefully curated to give you all the feels. It was also designed to open your mind and heart, remind you that you are not alone and that you need not sweat the small stuff. The stories that fill these pages are all incredibly different. Yet I see a piece of my own story in each of them, and I'm confident you will, too. A piece of myself exists in each of these women. We are so powerful when we band together and truly rise alongside one another. We have the ability to create real change in the world. But that change starts with us. It starts with a mental shift from comparison and judgment to acceptance and love. It entails reaching out, speaking up, and unapologetically standing by your intuition and conviction. We need not strive for perfection because we are all perfectly imperfect just the way we are. In the words of Brené Brown:

> *"Perfectionism is a self-destructive and addictive belief system that fuels this primary thought: If I look perfect, and do everything perfectly, I can avoid or minimize the painful feelings of shame, judgment, and blame."*

There it is. What we are all avoiding. Pain. Shame. Judgment. Guilt. Blame. Embarrassment. It is not perfectionism that will change this or start the movement — it is *us*. Each and every one of us. If we open our hearts to one another and genuinely come from a place of love and acceptance, then we become the change. I hope the next time those nagging questions or emotions creep in, or *She* speaks out of line, you reach out, speak up, and be real. Please just remember, wherever you are in your story, you've got this, Mama!

Section 1

THERE'S NO SUCH THING AS *PERFECT* TIMING

FEATURING

Bex Bucci

Sarah Secor-MacElroy

Habiba Jessica Zaman

Carrie Bruno

Cassie Jeans

OPENING COMMENTARY BY

Sabrina Greer

*H*ave you ever woken up in the morning feeling like you are stuck? Feeling like the wheels are turning but the vehicle isn't moving, or as though your feet are planted in quicksand? You know exactly what to do because the routine is set and you've done it nine thousand times before, but it still feels like you are waiting for something? Chasing the proverbial "if" and "when"? *If I get that job, then I will . . .* **When** *we move here, then we can . . .* **If** *I just reach this goal, then it will be the perfect time to . . .* **When** *I lose ten pounds, then I will buy that bathing suit.*

We are all guilty of this waiting game. Waiting for the *perfect* timing to make a change. This scenario likely rears its ugly head weekly, maybe even daily. This, my friends, is the Ego we were discussing earlier. She wants to keep you small, remember? It is human nature to want to be safe and to protect ourselves from danger. *She* tells us change is dangerous and works to keep us in that cozy little place known as our comfort zone.

When *should I become a mother?* When reflecting on this question and reading the chapters in this section, the answer is obvious to me now. However, it wasn't always so clear. Something I have definitely learned through my journey into motherhood is: There is never a *perfect* time for **anything**. This rings true for motherhood especially. We could always use more money, more time, less work, better health . . . you name your "reason" for holding out on whatever it is you're holding out on.

Did my journey into motherhood look the way I thought it would? Nope. Would I change a single thing now? No way! You see, it is okay to have these questions and doubts — it is okay because we are human and it's part of the journey. What we must do is realize that we are not the voices in our heads, we are just the ones who hear them.

What works for me is a concept that may be seen as new-age, trendy, maybe a little woo-woo — but, man, is it powerful. Ever heard of *surrendering?* **Surrender**. This does not mean quit, give up, or crumble to the floor. It means surrender — feel the feels, then release them gently. Let it go, whatever *it* is. In the words of a true surrender guru and one of my biggest inspirations, Michael Singer: *"Everything will be okay, once you are okay with everything. And that is the only time everything will be okay!"*

It is all about perspective. If we are always so inflexible and striving for perfection, it will never just be *okay*. There is never going to be a perfect time to become a mother. There is also no way to be a perfect mother; to your children, you will always be *their* perfectly imperfect mother. What matters is that you are a part of their life, their journey, and you have been given these children for a reason. Call it aligned timing, call it what you want: you have exactly what you need within you in order to be the best mother your children can have.

In the next five chapters, you will hear from women, much like myself, who struggled with figuring out *when* is the *perfect* timing. When I was with my previous partner, I remember saying things like, "When you get that promotion, I will go off birth control" and "When I finish my degree, we will get married." Thank goodness I surrendered to my imperfect life schedule! Because if we just surrender, it will all happen as it's meant to.

1

LIGHTING MY DARKNESS

by Bex Bucci

"I was writing the
book of my life,
& these were just
the chapters."

Bex Bucci

Bex is a spontaneous and energetic wife, mother, entrepreneur, and blogger. She lives in the suburbs of Chicago with her husband and their two wild and willful young daughters, Olivia and Eve.

Growing up, Bex never desired a traditional lifestyle for herself. She was a rebel against responsibility, obligation, and being tied down, so at age twenty-two, she vowed to never get married or have kids. She thoroughly enjoyed her freedom and had big dreams of becoming a best-selling author and moving to a posh apartment in New York City.

Although Bex *did* end up becoming a mother despite her plans, she is grateful for the positive impact it has had on her personal development. Her multi-passionate entrepreneurial spirit is something she hopes will inspire her daughters to chase their dreams.

Aside from being a mom, Bex has founded and run three successful ventures including a lingerie boutique, a positive body image campaign, and her current handmade candle business, *Happy Little Flame*. She has also recently launched a blog, *Her Brilliant Life*, which focuses on motherhood and identity.

fb: @happylittleflame | @herbrilliantlife
ig: @happy_little_flame | @herbrilliantlife

*"Not until we are lost do we begin to
understand ourselves."*
~ Henry David Thoreau

ello? Is there anyone out there? Can anyone hear me?
It felt as though I were shouting into an abyss, a black hole filled with children's laughter, tickles, snuggles, and overused phrases like "I love you to the moon and back" and "You're my world."

I was looking for someone — *anyone* — who felt how I felt, like they didn't belong.

It was hard enough being pregnant and hormonal, but not having anyone who could relate to me or offer support made me feel even more isolated.

I'd always had an aversion to kids and, more intensely, to the lifestyle of a parent. I thought I'd eventually develop a desire to have children, like most women . . . but it never happened. Not even a trace of maternal instinct existed in my being. The responsibility and obligation of parenthood repelled me so much, I was baffled as to why *anyone* would want to do it.

Throughout my twenties, while my friends and sisters were all getting married and having babies, there I was, boldly enjoying my freedom. The awareness I had of my unrestricted, independent lifestyle only grew stronger as more people in my circle became wives and mothers. It was as if the more responsibility they took on, the more I embraced and appreciated my freedom.

I met Sean (my husband) when I was twenty-six, smack in the middle of a decade-long party phase. He was so obviously meant for me — in the same phase, on the same level — and we instantly clicked. Be it weeknights or weekends, you'd find us at a party, a bar, or wherever shenanigans were happening. We had somehow found "home" together in these places, with these people . . . living nearly every moment on a whim, with spontaneity being our compass. Just how we wanted it.

Over the summer of 2012, something shifted within me, and I felt called to start a business. This is something I had never done before, but I forged forward, head first and excited. By November of that year, I found myself among hundreds of locals celebrating the grand opening of my new lingerie boutique. I had worked in the lingerie industry for eight years, but this adventure was certainly the most daring and brave thing I had embarked on. I was all in. This was it. This was my purpose.

I found parts of myself while working in that little shop on Center Street. It felt like a homecoming party — to myself. With every bra fitting, every conversation about self-worth and beauty, every mother-daughter bonding experience, I felt like I was discovering so many layers of myself that I hadn't realized before. The best part of starting my business? I was making a difference — I had the power to shape conversations, to help women and young girls feel beautiful, empowered, and confident about themselves, their souls, their bodies.

That winter Sean went back to school, which further shifted our focus from partying and living in the moment to our careers and professional development. As my business grew over the next couple of years, we found ourselves slowly drifting away from the party scene. We started enjoying things like cooking together, eating out, and hanging out at home watching TV shows and movies. In our own unique way, we had sort of grown up together.

Then, in February of 2015, I found out I was pregnant . . . and everything changed.

It was snowing hard that day. I believe we got two feet of snow — the heavy kind that sticks to everything it touches. It was Super Bowl Sunday, and Sean and I had just returned home from a family event and were expecting several guests at our condo to kick off our annual Super Bowl party. I was excited yet exhausted; I felt off that day. No, scratch that. I had felt "off" for weeks. My period was late as well.

Given the evening festivities, I was anticipating heavy drinking later that day, so I needed to make sure my intuition was wrong before getting totally sloshed. We decided to walk to the corner store and grab a pregnancy test since the roads were too awful to drive anywhere. We trudged through the snow back to our condo, and my stomach turned inside — flip-flopping and somersaulting — as I looked down at that bright pink box inside the plastic bag. We got home, and without even taking off my coat, I ran to the bathroom. Part of me didn't want to take a pregnancy test; I wanted to revel in the last few days of the wild life I had been living, loving. *Maybe I could just do it next week?* No. That certainly wasn't an option. I pulled out the box, did two tests at once — just to be sure.

I barely got the caps back on before the double lines appeared. My eyes welled. My body became heavy. That "off" feeling I'd had for weeks finally felt like a weight slowly settling onto my body. *I, freedom-bound, fun-loving, and carefree-living Rebekah, was pregnant. I was about to join the mom club.*

This thought kept circling in my mind and heart as I walked to the kitchen and pulled out the prepared food for our party. The more I thought about what was happening, the angrier I got. I was completely overwhelmed. I wanted to scream, sob, and vomit. It felt like too much was changing in a split second (or two minutes), thanks to the tests. I wanted someone to tell me it was a joke. That night, I sat on the couch sipping water and watched my friends enjoy themselves. I had to tell them I had a migraine and my eyes were watering from the pain, but really, I just wanted to cry the whole time. I ended up going to bed early and decided to give myself a few days. After the break from my newfound reality, Sean and I sat down to talk about how to handle this. We weighed the facts against my irrational hang-ups and emotions; I was thirty years old, I was with the man I knew was my soulmate. So why not go ahead with this? I loved him, he wanted to have kids, we were financially stable, and both of us were healthy.

Although moving forward with this pregnancy meant having to change *everything* about myself and my life, we went for it. For me, it felt like the "right" decision, the ultimate challenge . . . but deep down in my soul, with every fiber of my being — I didn't *want* it.

The months that followed were pure emotional agony. Physically, the only thing I struggled with was watching my body get bigger, which made me feel helpless, like I had lost all control over my life. I didn't endure any morning sickness, pain, illness, or any of the negative side effects that one might have during pregnancy. I literally had nothing to complain about. At least that's what it looked like on the surface. But deep within, *emotionally*, it was a war zone. It took every ounce of strength and courage I had to fight this horrific battle — desperately trying to convince myself that this was a good thing, while at the same time wishing it wasn't real. I was mourning my old life.

I spent hours upon hours scouring the internet looking for women like me: Women who felt they weren't meant to be moms, women who disliked children, and women who didn't want to have kids but had them anyway. I found nothing. Nada, zip, zilch. Absolutely nothing. I couldn't come up with a single resource. Not a single person. I even spoke to some friends and other moms about how I felt, hoping to gain some sense of normalcy and acceptance, but no one could relate. No one understood me. They all looked at me like I was crazy for not wanting children. *Was it that odd? Was I really the only one?* I had no one to talk to and felt isolated and alone. I felt scared. Terrified actually, but not only of the impending birth of a child I didn't want; I was afraid that these feelings would grow after she was born.

What if I couldn't handle motherhood? What if I screw up this little human because I'm not meant for this?

I needed an intervention, someone to smack sense into me and tell me I was being selfish and pessimistic, looking for excuses and having a pity party, when it didn't have to be that way at all. I didn't like the person I was becoming, and I hadn't even birthed my child yet. I knew I couldn't be a mom — certainly not a *good* one — unless something changed.

So I made a pact with myself that I would never let my child see, feel, or know how I felt. I would bury these feelings so deep inside of me, my child would never know they existed.

By the time my due date rolled around, I was beyond ready to get my life back. We had moved out of our condo and into a lake house earlier that spring, and I closed my boutique with a solid plan to re-open in a new location when the baby was old enough for daycare.

Olivia Mae was born on September 25, 2015, in the quickest, most painless delivery my doctor had ever seen. Or so she said.

The physical process was done. But . . . that was the easy part.

I was hoping I'd feel something emotionally. Excitement. Joy. Relief. I wanted to be one of those moms who entered the delivery room feeling one way and left feeling the opposite. I had hoped that a mother would somehow replace my former self. A *real* mother. With actual maternal feelings.

Then the nurses handed me this baby. *My* baby. She was perfect — she had ten fingers and ten toes, a full head of hair, and when I put her to my breast, she latched almost instantly. It was legitimately the most ideal scenario imaginable. Perfect birth. Perfect baby. Perfect mom? Nah, I don't think so — I felt nothing but sheer dread and anxiety.

I looked around the room, at the excited nurses, my grateful doctor, and my husband and mom, who were overcome with emotion. They were feeling *all* the things *I* should have been feeling. I studied them as though I were a robot trying to learn emotions, trying to get my cold, steel heart to feel something. Anything.

Why couldn't I feel anything?

When Sean went back to work, I didn't know what to do with myself. The days were so long and repetitive. I was trying to adjust to this new lifestyle — one I had spent my entire life trying to avoid — while running on no sleep, feeling lost, alone, and depressed. I had expected to feel this way; I'd always known motherhood wouldn't come to me easily. The weight of responsibility and obligation hung around my neck like a noose, its grip tightening with each day that passed.

As time went on, it dawned on me that everything I was experiencing came and went in phases. During a struggle or difficult time, I could look ahead to inevitable change. I knew brighter days would come. I was writing the book of my life, and these were just the chapters. Each chapter would end and another new one would begin. I was in control. I had the pen.

The Dark Years

As I emerged from misery and despair over the next several months, I felt as though I could finally breathe. At last, phew. I felt stronger, braver, more in control of my life and was gaining new confidence in myself with every day that passed.

One random evening in the middle of summer, just a few months before Olivia's first birthday, I realized that my period was late. On my way to the drugstore with a whiny ten-month-old in the back seat, I thought about how I would feel if I were pregnant again. That familiar feeling of dread immediately washed over me. But I was convinced I wasn't pregnant. *I couldn't be.*

When those two lines showed up on that pregnancy test, I didn't believe it. I took a second test, and when that one came back positive, I went back to the store to buy more. There was no freaking way. Over the course of the next couple of days I took seven tests. *Seven!* They were all positive.

My husband acted as though he were excited, but I could tell he was stressed. Not just about our future financial state, but because he knew how unhappy I was and how challenging the next several months (or years) would be.

And he was right. The following nineteen months were my personal living hell.

Eve Tyler was born on March 16, 2017, in a delivery similar to her sister's. I was induced at 8am and spent about ten hours on a super low-dose pitocin drip waiting for my doctor to have an opening, until they turned up the drip enough to actually induce labor at 6pm. By the time I had given birth (about fifteen minutes later), all I could think about was food. I was browsing through the hospital menu, ordering my celebratory meal not even two minutes after Eve was born.

Clearly, not much had changed.

However, things were much different this time around in terms of sleep. Eve was sleeping in her crib in her own room by two weeks old and only waking once (if that) at night. We breastfed for five months before we (Eve and I) mutually agreed it was time to call it quits. She loved to eat and sleep, unlike her sister.

But the days were long, and even though I was getting decent sleep most nights, I struggled to muster up the energy to play with my toddler. The struggle was more mental than physical. We did a ton of play dates, activities, and events outside the house because I couldn't be alone with my kids. Being at home made me feel lonely and isolated, just like I had felt when Olivia was a baby. I didn't have the mental capacity or the motivation to entertain my babies. I didn't *want* to play with them.

Truthfully, I didn't *want* to do anything. I had lost my enthusiasm for life; I had lost sight of my passions and dreams. More importantly, I lost myself in this process. Every morning, I felt heavy and tired. I was a shell of who I once was; no longer was I driven, motivated, or inspired. Every day, I wore a mask of perfect composure and a plastered smile, just for my babies, pretending I was interested and excited for our day together. The mom they knew was enthusiastic and happy. *That* was the mask I wore all day, every day. It was exhausting in a way I can't even explain.

I never considered that I may have been dealing with postpartum depression (PPD) with either pregnancy. I was convinced that the reason I felt so down was because I didn't want to be a mom. I thought this would be my life forever: struggling through each day, doing something I didn't want to be doing.

I still didn't have anyone to talk to, nor could I find the support I needed to get through this. I kept swimming, barely managing to keep my head above water . . . hoping someone would eventually see me and pull me out. But nobody saw me.

Surprisingly, despite the yucky feeling of constant resentment, I felt like I was a good mom. Oftentimes, a great mom. Not because of the sacrifices I had made, the things I gave up for my kids, or even the fact that I was silently fighting this battle, but rather because I was aware. I was paying attention to every detail about the things my girls were experiencing and feeling. I was present for them, mentally, emotionally, and physically. I was consciously making an effort to do things I didn't want to do, with enthusiasm. For *them*.

Right around Olivia's second birthday in September 2017, another shift took place.

Eve was six months old, and we were entering a new phase of life. My girls were becoming more independent, and with that, my stress and anxiety levels began dissipating. I found myself becoming excited when I'd look ahead to the future, knowing things just might get easier from here.

I was scrolling through Instagram one morning (before the girls were awake), and I came across this page that just pulled me in. This woman was right around my age, married, with two kids, and running a successful handmade business. Her life looked so fun and fulfilling. But it also somehow looked attainable. *Could I do something like this? Could I run a business and be a mom? Could I have this life?*

In that moment, my passion, drive, and enthusiasm for life came rushing back. There was a fire in my belly, and my heart was racing a mile a minute. I felt something I hadn't in a long time. Hope!

A few weeks later, I found myself in my kitchen buried in supplies, teaching myself how to make candles. I had no idea what I was doing, but I knew my end goal, my mission.

Over the course of the next few months, I spent every naptime, evening, and weekend experimenting, testing, and perfecting my product. I became completely obsessed with this new project. I woke up each morning with that old familiar fire in my belly and passion in my eyes. My motivation and enthusiasm for life was returning. I felt alive again!

But along with the highs of this new endeavor came the lows.

A new kind of resentment grew in me as my desire to spend more time working on my business was challenged every day by my responsibility as a stay-at-home mother. I often found myself thinking, *I would so much rather be working on my business right now* or *If I didn't have kids, I could be doing so much more.* I was almost angry at my kids for not allowing me to pursue my passions the way I wanted to, when I wanted to, how I wanted to. I felt like my fire was being smothered yet again, but in a more intense way. Because *this* was exactly why I didn't want kids.

In January 2018, Sean and I decided to hire a babysitter two full days a week so I could get a grip on my goals and focus on growing my business.

This. Was. Life-changing. It was magical, my lifeline back to myself.

I had no idea how much I needed this time for myself, even if it was solely intended for work. The break I got from "momming" almost instantly catalyzed an unexpected journey of self-discovery and growth for me. *This* was what I had been searching for, what my heart had been seeking, and what I needed on that snowy Super Bowl Sunday almost two years ago. I didn't need someone who understood me or someone who was fighting the same battle I was. Nor did I need support or encouragement from others. I needed *me*. I needed unwavering belief in myself. I needed courage and strength, from the inside. *I* was there all along, I just had to learn to connect with myself again and trust my intuition.

Looking back on these influential years of my life, I can't say I regret a single thing. Even in those times of darkness and depression, I not only survived, I thrived in my role as a mother. I was aware, thoughtful, and intentional with my children — even at my absolute worst. *That* in itself gave me an immeasurable sense of confidence, which was the missing piece I needed to begin my journey and fully accept myself as a mother. Working through your internal demons can be a scary and ugly thing, especially when they involve precious beings like your children.

I don't love being a mom. Yes, I have no qualms admitting that, even now. But I love my kids with every fiber of my being, and I thank God for them every single day. I wouldn't be who I am, or where I am at this moment, had it not been for them. They are more important to me than anything in this world, and I will keep working hard so they never, ever have to question my love for them.

~ For the moms out there who never wanted kids but had them anyway, and my daughters Liv & Eve; never, ever be afraid to live your truth.

2

THE MAGICAL THINKING PARADOX

by Sarah Secor-MacElroy

"Unconditional love is what we crave: to be accepted as and for who we are."

Sarah Secor-MacElroy

Sarah Secor-MacElroy is an original member of The Mama Tribe, having contributed to the first book in the *You've Got This, Mama* series. Motherhood was not something Sarah aspired to, but the birth of her first son guided her toward her life's purpose. Sarah shares her musings about raising three sons and overcoming anxiety on her blog, Mother of Wildthings, and is a regular contributor for the YGTMAMA blog. Sarah's debut children's book, *Leaping Lumberjacks*, a brave book about always being yourself, is due to be released on the Golden Brick Road imprint in 2019. In addition to being an author, Sarah recently launched a clothing brand and online store, The Wild Life, with her husband Drew. Sarah has always desired to design clothing, but it was living through the fourth trimester with a very different post-twin pregnancy body that provided the spark of inspiration. She felt there was a gap in the market for women transitioning out of maternity apparel, with new curves and new needs. She endeavored to create clothing that would make other mothers and all women feel good about themselves. The brand has grown to include men's, women's, children's and infant apparel, with a focus on coordinating pieces for the whole family.

www.motherofwildthings.com | www.shopthewildlife.net
ig: @Mother_of_Wildthings

"You are a marvel. You are unique. In all the years that have passed, there has never been another child like you. Your arms, your legs, your clever fingers, the way you move. You may become a Shakespeare, a Michelangelo, a Beethoven. You have the capacity for anything."

~ Henry David Thoreau

My husband brings me coffee almost every morning, something I don't always recognize as being special until there isn't a cup waiting for me when I wake up. It is a simple gesture, occasionally overlooked, but I realize how sweet it is and always try to thank him once I am fully awake. I casually mentioned this to a friend once, and she immediately lamented the things her husband did not do for her, comparing her marriage to mine. My intent was never to boast about what my spouse did or to make her feel bad; I wanted to share something with her and, in a small way, to celebrate how he treats me.

This is something that happens often — we compare our loved ones to other people and shine a light on their perceived shortcomings instead of exalting their unique individuality. I am guilty of this, too. I have three sons and often compare them to each other: the twins to one another and then the twins to their older brother when he was their age. I try to be mindful of this and stop myself because they are three wonderfully different little boys; I should instead spend my time praising their individuality and focusing on ways I can help each of them thrive and reach their individual highest potential.

As parents we all desire for our children to be fiercely independent and unapologetically unique, yet so often we hold them to unrealistic expectations instead of allowing them to be who they are meant to be at specific life stages: themselves. When we require a toddler to behave like an adolescent, or when we expect a teenager to have the emotional maturity of an adult, we are placing unrealistic and not age-appropriate expectations onto them. We all have aspirations and ambitions for our children, but it becomes a hindrance to our relationship with them when we cannot let go of our desires for their lives and allow them to discover and cultivate their own. Expectations must be tempered to align with reality; in doing this, we will lessen the chances of feeling let down.

The principles I am addressing here apply to many aspects of life, especially relationship dynamics. When we compare our relationships to others, it is like ingesting poison. It sows the seeds of discontentment, which leads to disappointment and resentment. Like necrosis, it will eat away at the healthy tissue, leaving you with only devastation. For instance, when we look at other marriages and wonder why our spouse *doesn't* do what someone else does or isn't as funny, charming, wealthy, or whatever as someone else's spouse, we are thinking from a place of discontent instead of from our heart. There will always be someone funnier, wealthier, healthier, more intelligent, or more attractive — *always*. I am not suggesting that anyone settle for less here, but I am suggesting that we learn to appreciate what we have.

We have become desensitized to how much we compare our children to one another and gauge their abilities and aptitudes, sometimes by wholly made-up scales. We do not realize how detrimental it can be to the parent-child relationship, to their psyche and being. On the surface, the grass may seem greener elsewhere, but we forget that some people have Astro-Turf and others might use toxic chemicals to artificially stimulate theirs.

I often imagine how events will unfold or how experiences will be. I overthink and overanalyze; I have what my husband refers to as "Paris syndrome." After living in Germany for about a year, we drove to Paris over a long weekend. I had dreamed of traveling to Paris since I was a young girl, and I still held onto some of these fantastical ideas as an adult. I imagined Paris would be a Mecca of posh, sophisticated, Chanel-clad women — but everywhere we went, it was just heaps of tourists in overalls (no offense to the overall-wearing people of the world) and air so thick you needed to chew it. Eventually I did snap out of my discontentment and enjoy the rest of our trip, but my manufactured expectations forever marred part of this wonderful experience. I often imagine how every detail of an event will be, and then lo-and-behold, the truth sinks in: I have three children under the age of six. I am quickly brought back to my reality, usually by something being hurled at my head, by one of them yelling, or by someone bleeding.

Recently we decided all the kids were old enough to go on a family bike ride. Oh how wrong we were. In my mind, the scene played out like a commercial: the sun was shining, my three blonde boys looked adorable in their shiny new helmets, the babies were in a cool bike trailer pod, and my oldest was on his brand new bike. Our ride got off to a great start — everyone was dressed and on a bike! Half way around a lake, my oldest son spotted dandelions and cool sticks and immediately hopped off his bike, dropped it to the ground, and ran toward them. He was over the bike ride completely and had absolutely zero interest in riding his bike anymore. To my husband, this was insubordination, willful disobedience; to me, this was a five-year-old who wanted cool sticks for a sandbox battle between Optimus Prime and Darth Vader. Our son, meanwhile, was blissfully unaware that he had upset anyone else's plans. This was a perfect example of needing to adjust our expectations to meet reality. You might be a "rose-colored glasses" type, and that is okay — not only okay, it is wonderful! Optimism is a trait to nurture and cherish; however, unbridled wishful or "magical thinking," as my father calls it, will lead to disappointment when your expectations do not align with the world around you. Being discontented with one's family or situation is a tale as old as time; take, for example, the parable of The Prodigal Son from the Bible.

We as a culture have become even further obsessed with a picture-perfect, filtered, and distorted existence. That world, however, does not exist. Theodore Roosevelt once said, and as Sabrina mentions in the introduction, "Comparison is the thief of joy," and that couldn't have been truer. At some stage of our parenting journey, we have two choices: to allow our children the freedom to be who they are intended to be and embrace who they are or to stifle them with our unrealized dreams, desires, or perfectionist expectations. These choices can have lifelong implications and can shape the trajectory of the parent-child relationship, cementing either a loving, open, secure attachment or one filled with resentment, anxiety, and insecurity. I don't mean to make all of this sound so easy; it can be exceedingly painful to let go of the expectations we have created for our children's lives as they differentiate and become individuals.

I was an 80s baby, and my mother lived to dress my brother and me up in matching Laura Ashley outfits. She was so very proud of us and wanted everyone to know she was our mother. This was all well and good when I was four years old; however, I began making it clear I didn't like the dresses. I used to twist the buttons off (while wearing them out), and I was even known to toss my shoes out of a car window when I didn't feel like being a little dress-up doll. This drove my mother crazy, as she had painstakingly curated coordinating family outfits and couldn't fathom why I did not like them, too. They were the things she dreamed of owning and wearing as a child. The key word here is *she* — these were not my dreams, they were hers. This was the first time I exercised my independence, slowly forging my way and growing into a very defiant and strong-willed person (much to my parents' and now husband's ire).

This independence will serve our children well in adulthood, but we seem to want to squash this character trait in our children to make things easier on us. It is our desire to save our children from suffering that can push us to act in a way that may stifle their individuality. Some parents have rules about appearances, like *no purple hair under this roof* or *no son of mine will pierce his ears*. But these simple acts of youthful rebellion have no long-term consequences (other than maybe some stained towels and an ear infection if the piercing is not done hygienically). My suggestion is not to change your core values or abandon all principles, but to remember what it feels like to be young and impetuous. Remember all the angst and faux romance that swirls all around you as a teenager, not to mention the situations you magnify in your mind.

Perhaps you were never impetuous; instead you were always cautious and calculated, and you cannot understand your wild child. Try. Try to understand what pushes them, what they love, what they don't love, and who they want to be. Find common ground of any kind.

My parents and I had nothing in common, but my dad made an effort to understand *why* I liked heavy metal music. He was into The Beatles, Jethro Tull, and The Who, and both he and my mother spent their evenings attending the symphony — an alternate universe from the death metal and other music I enjoyed. My father tried to bridge the gap; he printed out lyrics he couldn't understand, we spent hours debating the meanings, and occasionally he ventured out to concerts with me. It was not something he ever thought he would do or enjoy, and he never grew to like the music, but he made the effort and ended up forging a strong bond and creating memories with me I will carry forever.

We also must push our children to reach their full potential while being a loving and positive force in their life. If you are not the person influencing your child's choices, believe me, someone else will be, and it may not always be a healthy influence. I grew up watching Baywatch, and my idol was Pamela Anderson. This was not the role model my parents wanted me to have. Eventually, I grew out of this phase, but not before it left a lasting impression on me. It imprinted on my young mind the power of sex appeal and the idea that women were merely here to be pretty, not powerful. Now I am not knocking Pam as a human being (to each their own), but I want my sons role models to be my husband and me, my father and mother, and the kinds of people around them who are positively shaping the world. I want my boys to know that strength comes from within — not from your physical presence, but rather the strength of your character and the power of your will.

We must push our children's boundaries with positive reinforcement and encouragement to promote healthy and well-adjusted development while simultaneously not infringing on their individuality. We can decide when it is time to move past pacifiers and bottles, to learn to swim or ride a bike, but we must also cultivate an awareness to know which of their boundaries should not be pushed.

Parenting is complicated, and we must navigate the seasons of our children's growth and development with love, kindness, patience, and understanding. We can learn to accept and celebrate our children for who they are, to walk alongside them on their journey even when their path diverges from what we would have envisioned or chosen for them. My parents never expected that my life would involve some of the things it did: running off with bands as a teenager, tattooing my entire back, or marrying a biker (you have to read the first book for that story). None of that is something you dream your precious newborn will aspire to do someday. But my parents loved me unconditionally and accepted me back every time, without fail, when I ran off and made wild decisions or did things they didn't understand. When their friends and other family members told them that the best thing to do was let me go or cut me off, they persisted. *"Children need love especially when they seem to not deserve it."*[1]

I walked a road that my parents never could have conjured up in their worst nightmares. For years, I tried to distance myself from my family because I thought my burdens were too painful for them to bear. Children worry just like we do, and most children never want to let their parents down. When I was a freshman in college, my father was just three years removed from having cancer and coming so incredibly close to dying. I watched him wither and accept his inevitable fate and I watched my mother try to keep it together and not lose hope. During this phase of our lives, I kept anything difficult, sad, or painful to myself because I thought in my teenage brain they couldn't handle anything else. As an adult, I now know this is untrue. I now understand that the depth of our feelings and love for our children cannot be measured in any capacity and that we can handle so much more than we even know. I lived through years of trauma and abuse, and I retreated into alcoholism to cope. Adulthood is when I mustered the strength to open up about all the trauma I had endured silently, and *that* day was the biggest epiphany for my parents. They finally understood why I made some of the choices I did. Many children and young adults will shut down when parents pry, and I know this is a precarious place, but never give up. Change your approach or tactics. Even when children seem too old or to not care, remind them how much you love them and how precious they are; even if they roll their eyes or dismiss you, they hear you.

---

1   Katz, L., & Tello, J. (2003). "I love me!" How to nurture self-esteem. Scholastic Parent and Child, 10(6).

My parents let me fail when I needed to, they let me learn hard lessons that were equally hard for them, many times. As parents, we want to prevent our children from experiencing pain and suffering, but unfortunately, this isn't a realistic long-term goal. We can try to protect our babies and toddlers from the dangers in our homes — we buy light socket covers, we lock up dangerous chemicals, and we warn them of stranger danger. But at some point, so much earlier than any of us are ready for, we have to allow them to be independent of us. We can't make decisions for our children forever; at some point we have to step back and let them make their own choices. Much of the power struggle that occurs between strong-willed children and their parents is because we, as parents, are expecting our children to be like us, to make choices the way we do, to be who *we* think they should be.

Where we derive these expectations from has much to do with our own past and the baggage we carry with us from our own childhood and upbringing — the good and bad. Children pick up on their parents' subconscious tendencies; maybe you don't even realize some of the things you say about yourself, but I bet your spouse / partner and your children do. As adults, so many of us walk around with wounds from our pasts, some gaping and still raw and some buried a little deeper. What we put out into the world, intentionally or unintentionally, will be reflected at our children. Anger, substance abuse, anxiety, depression, vulgarity, infidelity — these are heavy burdens for any adult to bear, but they are excruciating burdens for children. Our children can be a mirror that we may not want to look into. We must make amends with the past and accept ourselves as we are, thus enabling us to become unburdened in our interactions in our interactions. We must strive to find contentment within ourselves and in our lives. The examples we live by speak so much louder than the words we say to our children. We may tell our children they are beautiful, but what are we saying about ourselves? We may advise them to respect others but fail to realize that we fall short of that regularly. It is these discrepancies that children pick up on.

Use positive affirmations daily to help yourself and your children understand the transformative power of positivity and to teach them how to treat themselves. Children should be exposed not only to our strength but also to our fragility and humanity We must instill in our children and ourselves that we are not without mistakes and that we are still worthy of redemption. It is our sacred responsibility to remind our children of this throughout their lifetime.

It is never too late to make a change; all you have to do is decide you want something to be different. Do you and your spouse argue in front of your kids and you don't want to do that anymore? Make a change. Do you compare your children's aptitudes to one another, not realizing that you may be causing sibling rivalry? Make a change. Every day we make countless choices, and if you don't like how things went yesterday, then change them. If you don't like the parenting style you have settled into, change it. We are only stuck if we give up.

We long to connect with others, and the most fundamental of these connections is with our parents. To know we are loved and accepted by them is crucial. We will face many challenges throughout the parenting life cycle — from a birth that doesn't go as planned to a physical or medical issue we never expected to an adolescent with an attitude problem. This wheel keeps moving on into adulthood; it is not just toddlers and adolescents who make us scratch our heads and wonder *why?* Love, unconditional love, is what we crave; to be accepted as we are and for who we are is what we need. Every child is a gift, a lesson; embrace and accept the child(ren) you have! Embrace and accept yourself and the journey that brought you to where you are today. Choose joy and choose love always.

~To my parents John and Sandy,
thank you for never giving up on your wild child.

3

LEARNING TO LOVE MYSELF

by Habiba Jessica Zaman

"Let go of what your life should look like and celebrate it for what it is."

Habiba Jessica Zaman

Habiba Jessica Zaman, NCC LPC, has a master's degree in professional counseling specializing in trauma and is the therapist and owner at North Star of Georgia Counseling. With fifteen years of work experience in the counseling field, including counseling, advocacy, guidance, and education, she believes that as awareness of one's fears, perception, desires, and strengths increases, one can make successful life changes. Increasing our self-awareness through becoming more honest with ourselves can initiate the authenticity that often results in healing, transformation, and a fuller life. Habiba has thirteen publications that started with a children's book, *But I'm Just Playing*, in 2012; her latest co-authored works, *Beautifully Bare, Undeniably You* and the original *You've Got This, Mama*, were released in 2018. Habiba is of Bangladeshi and American descent. She has two children and lives in Atlanta, Georgia with her family.

www.habibazaman.com
ig: @habibti_zaman
fb: habibajessicazaman | northstarofgeorgiaauthenticity

*"Self-love, self-respect, self-approval, and self-worth
do not equal selfish."*
~ Mandy Hale

P hysically, emotionally, mentally depleted . . . is an understatement.
I find myself in these situations from time to time. Some days I am
fighting this sense of dread or just feeling low, while other days, I let
myself fall face first into a deep, dark hole. Many people encounter this kind
of struggle, whether it's due to the loss of a job or some other kind of loss,
a major life change like a birth or growth of a family, or just daily issues taking their toll. By the end of the day, we no longer have anything left to give
and don't want to do the things we would typically enjoy, such as reading or
meeting with friends.

I have become increasingly aware that almost everyone I know, including
myself, is incredibly busy. It's almost as though we hide behind "busy-ness"
as a badge of honor. Some of my friends work sixty-plus hours a week while
raising their children, driving all over the country to further their careers,
and, to top it all off, maintaining their social life as well. With our schedules
packed so tight, I began to ponder, how do we make time for ourselves?

*"Sometimes you don't realize you are drowning
when you are trying to be everyone else's anchor."*
~ Anonymous

Studies show that when we become extremely stressed or run down, our bodies can react to these emotions. Our bodies show the signs of chronic stress both physically and mentally. When we keep ourselves so busy, not only is it difficult to be our most productive selves, it can also lead to an unbalanced life. We are running here and there, taking care of the new baby (or babies), playing chauffeur to our other children, completing a new project (whether work or home), meeting that deadline . . . the list is endless.

As women, we have the physical workload both at home and at work, but we also carry the mental and emotional workload — taking care of everyone around us, every little detail and appointment. But who exactly ensures we take care of ourselves? The answer is . . . no one but us. It is entirely up to us to prioritize self-care on our checklist.

First, it is important to listen to our body and be aware of signals that let us know we are feeling overwhelmed and need to take a break. For some of us, we may notice that we become more irritable and less social; others may have physical symptoms of stress, such as hives or uncontrollable eye twitches. When we recognize these signs, we can plan for self-care. Stop what you are doing and take five deep breaths. HALT (Hungry Angry Lonely and Tired) is an acronym commonly used in the field of psychotherapy for awareness and time to take action. When you are dealing with one or more of these symptoms simultaneously, you may be your own worst enemy and can fall victim of your subconscious. Self-deprecating messages can run rampant, and the likelihood of responding to a situation rather than *reacting* to it is slim to none.

Sleep . . . when was the last time I had a complete night of sleep? Ten years ago, while the eldest was in my belly? Sleep. That sounds heavenly. I am sitting here at piano practice after six long sessions at the office, listening to the boys learn their songs, and I find myself drifting into la-la land. Status: Mentally? I'm drained. Physically? I'm done. Emotionally? Glitching like my phone. Spiritually? Barely hanging on. I saw a meme earlier and started laughing hysterically because it said something like, "I'm not an early bird or a night owl . . . I am some form of permanently exhausted pigeon." YES! Yes, that is what I am. I am depleted on every level, and I wonder how I got here? I have had restless sleep for the past three days because I am just so far past exhausted. I feel like a two-year-old who needed a nap an hour ago and is flailing around on the floor because she can't settle. My shoulders feel as though they are holding bricks up to my ears, and I swear to you, my clients can see that twitch in my left eye. Where is that vivacious mama and powerful queen? I am her; she is somewhere inside. On the outside I look the part, but the inside doesn't match at all. I am not a true reflection of the sea of turmoil threatening to drown me. And thank goodness for that! That in itself is a double-edged sword. I don't look sickly and feverish, so the demands keep coming. "Mom, can you do this? Mom, can you get that? Mom, can we go here? Mom, mama, mommy, amma, mamai, maman!" And I look over and smile, saying yes. Yes, even though I need a moment. Yes, even though I really need to eat lunch and it is 3pm. Yes, my love, even though I could really use a thirty-minute nap. Yes to the dishes, yes to the laundry, yes to the vacuum . . . What does it say about me as a single mother and businesswoman if it's not all put together? Am I a failure? This is so hard . . . When do I get a chance? When will I say yes to me?

Second, once we have gained an awareness of our body's signals, it is helpful to have a list of activities that replenish us and help us to get back to a balanced and fulfilled state.

"The difference between try and triumph is a little 'umph'."
~ Unknown

There are countless studies on how exercise enhances the chemicals in the brain that impact positive mood. I should just tell you now, I *despise* structured exercise. I loathe the treadmill, the elliptical, and any other machine that makes me feel like I am a hamster running in a wheel, chasing my imagined sense of freedom. However, what I do *love* is dancing. There is always music playing every morning once I wake up, while I am getting the kids and myself ready for the day, as I am driving to work, on my way home from work, and as I am cleaning up at day's end. I am that person in the car next to you shimmying without a care in the world to unheard music. I am the paradox who is rapping to the cats one moment and waltzing to Ed Sheeran's *Perfect* with my sons the next. But let's say dancing is not your thing. We can fit movement in with more creative avenues, if you are like me and try to find any excuse to avoid an actual trip to the gym. Take a long walk around a trail at a park or your neighborhood or office complex. Take a hike with or without the family and just let the sunshine hit your face. Check out other movement classes offered around the city. The options are plenty if we just look outside the box.

"We travel not to escape life, but for life not to escape us."

~ Anonymous

Sometimes it takes a literal change in perspective to change our mental perspective. My form of literal change is an escape; I live for new experiences and adventures. I'm sure it sounds daunting, but it's true. Every two to three months, I get the escape itch, yearning for my next fun adventure or getaway. It could be a spontaneous trip to the beach or a few miles away to a new part of town to explore. Sometimes it's taking a new route home when I am stuck in traffic. My two boys have learned to understand the meaning when I say, "Let's have an adventure." As my nine-year-old son so lovingly put it, "You're deliberately going to get lost now, Mama, aren't you?" Although routine and responsibility can be calming because they provide structure and predictability, they can also stifle the person we once were before we had this wonderful life we created for ourselves. Each transformation and transition is an extension of who we are, and yet many of us lose touch with who we once were.

"Stick with the people who pull the magic out of you and not the madness." ~ Anonymous.

The magnificent collection of stories in this book reflect the heart and soul of an empowered village. We **can** do it all alone, but imagine what we could accomplish when we are able to share the load with those trusted members of our tribe? It is vital to have a support system we can lean on and share our experiences as a mother / wife / sister / daughter / lover. In a society heavily indulgent in social media and my personal best friend and nemesis Pinterest, we still need the raw, unfiltered, authentic versions of what it means to be a woman. Our addiction to perfection — perfect appearances, perfect lives, perfect mother / wife / sister / friend / lover / boss /

colleague — needs a reality check. We need moments when we can ugly cry while laughing hysterically at the beautiful train wreck called life. We need to surround ourselves with people and conversations that leverage enthusiasm, excitement, and satisfaction. We need to spend time with people who build us up, see and encourage our strengths, and who are, themselves, living their life intentionally and authentically.

"Happiness is not something you postpone for the future; it is something you design for the present." ~ Jim Rohn

Often we feel unfulfilled with our lives because we are not *living*; we are simply functioning on autopilot. Let go of what your life *should* look like and celebrate it for what it is. I feel that as each year goes by and we become more reliant on technology, we are losing our ability to be mindful of ourselves and our surroundings. We are losing our awareness of how things affect us and our feelings. We have this tendency to live in our heads, fixating on what happened in the past or feeling anxious about what is coming, without paying attention and experiencing *this* moment. If we lose the ability to be aware of and put a name to our experiences, we cannot process, explore, or cope; this ultimately leads us back into the "hole" or rut. Over time, we become numb to the little bits of joy that surround us. Just in the past ten minutes, I've been able to witness both joy and pride as I write this chapter and as I watch my boys regurgitate messages I've taught on repeat, as one says to the other, "Be supportive, Ryu, not critical."

"I have learned that as long as I hold fast to my beliefs and values — and follow my own moral compass — then the only expectations I need to live up to are my own." ~ Michelle Obama

We are satisfied with our existence when it is congruent and reflective of our values. How do we identify these values? It helps when you follow your intuition and ask yourself whether something is important to you. We usually categorize a list of values as crucial, necessary, and unimportant. What are some crucial aspects in our life, relationships, and roles we play? Have faith you will be supported the more you authentically reveal yourself. Identify and envision the life you wish to have, which includes a blueprint of the roles you would like to play in this world you have created for yourself. Identifying our values also teaches us why we respond to situations the way we do. When a value is violated, we have an automatic negative reaction. Our values come from our world view, which is determined based on needs that were met or not met in our childhood. When we know our values and can identify where they come from, we can then answer *why* something is a big deal for us. That is the only way we can learn to ask for what is important for us, whether it's asking it from those close to us or even asking from ourselves.

Look within to find your values; once you do, figure out how they are put into action so that you are living your most authentic life. Start taking steps, large or small, to make these values your reality. Stay in touch with who you are. Align yourself to your thoughts, feelings, and actions. Stay fully present to who you are and what you would like to achieve.

Change . . . So much change. At times, I am floating, flying, and falling free while on other days I feel broken and completely alone. This tearing apart of what was once my norm will make way for me to piece back the puzzle that makes up my existence in order to reflect what I have always longed for. This is my chance to create and manifest the life I deserve, one that mirrors the person I am on the inside. It is important because I know that to some, I am an enigma. A quote from Rumi that's dear to me states, "Study me as much as you like, you will never know me. For I differ a hundred ways from what you see me to be. Put yourself behind my eyes, and see me as I see myself. Because I have chosen to dwell in a place you can't see."

I see myself indulging in wanderlust, taking in the culture, people, history, and, most importantly cuisine from all over the world. Walking arm in arm, filled with wonder, passion, and adventure with someone who shares this same thirst.

I see nights spent wrapped up in that other person, open, naked, and vulnerable; completely consumed by fire and desire — utterly exposed and unhindered sexuality. I see a partner who will make me laugh, smile, grow, lust, want, crave, be proud of what I have accomplished and who I am, while encouraging me to keep growing. I see deep conversations and an understanding of my ideas and perspectives, whether he accepts it or not. I see someone who is willing to share my responsibilities, making me feel safe and secure. More importantly, he will continue to let me know I am not alone; we are together, two beings unafraid to unfurl their wings and revel in their individuality while still coming together as one, no matter what. I see freedom, where I have the security of knowing that I have a choice in directing the trajectory of my life in the areas of work, friendships, and interests, without the fear of consequence or punishment from my partner. I see a man who views the world from a similar lens, with whom just being and co-existing is effortless. I see a man who brings love, joy, affection, and empathy. Someone who continuously challenges me to grow and reach my full potential and who is open and secure enough to grow with me. Not only that, he is empowered by my knowledge and understanding of the world. I want it to be instinctive — the way he falls for me. Like an effortless intake of breath.

I see Sunday brunch surrounded by those who can see past the façade and accept all I am, all that makes me undeniably, me. Brunches filled with laughter, children, friendships, genuine connection, and ease of being. Brunches filled with delicious food, wine, and desserts. Always with an air of deep regard and authentic conversations.

With my children, I see strong bonds and secure attachments, an unspoken understanding of emotional safety and unconditional acceptance of one another. I see inside jokes and late night calls to announce life-changing milestones. They will come to me with their heartbreaks, and I will hold them while they share their deepest fears and concerns. I see playful banter and intellectual conversations, forever challenging each other to learn and grow. I see family vacations and an expansion of our little unit.

Finally, maintain a commitment to leading a balanced life. I can tell you from firsthand experience that this is so much easier said than done, but we must try. Don't be afraid to ask for help; remember that we are not super humans and that it is a sign of strength to ask for assistance when you know you need it. Remember to slow down. Plan relaxation and meditation into your day, even for a few minutes, no matter how busy you are. Relax your standards and reduce overwhelming demands and responsibilities. The most common triggers correspond to the acronym HALT — when you feel hungry, angry, lonely, or tired. Take care of yourself, mentally and physically, to ward off these triggers. Get plenty of sleep. Fatigue is a stressor. Rank scenarios as low, medium, or high risk for you. It's crucial to have this free time in your schedule so you can recharge for the next week. Our brains are wired for love, connection, and cooperation. But the individualism, social isolation, and competition of modern society have led to imbalance within ourselves, in our relationships, and with nature. We see the results in current epidemics of anxiety, loneliness, pain, and obesity. Dr. Kristin Neff, in *Self-Compassion: The Proven Power of Being Kind to Yourself*, shared, "Self-compassion is a more constant personal quality, in which we value ourselves and treat ourselves kindly just because we are human. And this caring attitude to ourselves helps us to recognize our similarity and connection with other humans, who share with us common aspirations and sources of suffering." Be gentle with yourself and learn who you are so you can care for yourself as you deserve to be cared for. As Max Ehrmann so beautifully articulated, "In the noisy confusion of life, keep peace in your soul."

~ I dedicate this chapter to my two amazing boys,
Ryu and Luca, who helped teach me that not only
do they deserve the best version of mama,
but that in order to be able to give them that,
I first have to recognize that I am worthy
of loving myself, too.

4

FINDING JOY IN UNEASE

by Carrie Bruno

"As parents, we need to model the behavior we want to see in our children."

Carrie Bruno

Carrie is founder of *The Mama Coach*, a Registered Nurse, and an IBCLC lactation consultant. She is a proud mama of two beautiful boys, Griffen and Mikale. They are her everything, although she now knows that putting her own oxygen mask on first only benefits her family. Her husband Cody was the first entrepreneur in the family, encouraging Carrie to take the plunge and follow her heart. Carrie describes him as the most encouraging and supportive man on the planet.

It feels ironic to Carrie that she is co-authoring a book, as she vividly remembers her mom pulling her off centre field during her fastball game after reading the essay Carrie completed hurriedly to make it to the game. But ever since she was a little girl, she was always up for a challenge or for something new. Caring for people is in her essence, so nursing came naturally. When life changed and she didn't feel happy anymore, her bravery, along with encouragement from her husband, helped create the nationwide company, *The Mama Coach*. Her writing has been featured in *Mother.ly*, and *Today's Parent*. She has also been featured on the *W Network* in Bachelorette Jillian Harris's hit reality TV show, teaching Jillian's prenatal class, and has been named one of Calgary's Top 40 under 40 in 2018. Carrie derives joy from being with family; her sister and cousins are her besties. If you need her, she is most likely in the arena, Tim Hortons drink in hand, watching her little guys play hockey.

www.themamacoach.ca
ig: @the.mama.coach
fb: themamacoachcalgary

Photo credit: @rhodesjamen

*"Vulnerability is the birthplace of innovation,
creativity and change."*

~ Brené Brown

I had coffee on my mind as we newlyweds drove through the tiny town of Armstrong, British Columbia, Canada. It was July, and my husband and I had just gotten married the week before. We were spending the next seven days exploring the beauty of BC, with big plans for a Hawaiian honeymoon during fall of that same year. I hadn't been feeling one hundred percent the last few days, and I felt sweaty when I realized that my period was late. I looked at Cody, who was driving with one arm out the window, listening to the playlist he made for our trip. I told him my period was late, and he looked at me all confused, as if I was speaking another language. The coffee shop we stopped at had a drugstore next to it, so I ran in, bought a test, and saw two pink lines appear in the coffee shop bathroom not even five minutes later.

Oh my word. I left the washroom to see my tourist husband with our new camera (wedding gift) in his hand, balancing our lattes. He took one look at my face and dropped our coffees, along with our new camera. The cement floor became a mix of shattered camera glass and coffee. We sat in silence on the bench outside the coffee shop.

I was pregnant.

We hadn't been super careful about contraception but definitely weren't actively trying to start a family. We were just a few days into our mini-honeymoon when we chose to turn around our (two passenger) truck and head straight for home. It was a quiet ride back to Alberta as we both reflected on how our lives were about to change.

I am a labor and delivery registered nurse (RN) and have always been passionate about supporting women through the birth process. It was only natural for me to feel confident as my belly grew; I worked with moms and babies for a living. Surely I knew how to do this. Boy, was I wrong! I feel like I worried about a lot of stuff. My anatomical ultrasound took an extra thirty minutes because I insisted the technician show me all four chambers of the baby's heart, his palate, even the lenses in his eyes!

But I never once worried about sleep. I remember telling my family, "I'm a shift worker, staying up with a baby won't bother me at all." *Famous last words.*

Fast forward to the postpartum unit. It forever changed our lives when we met our son, Griffen, after a fast labour. The next morning, I held eight pounds of beautiful boy, dressed in the sweater my grandma made for him, as I waited for Cody to come pick us up. He had hurried home to "quickly" install the car seat. Three hours later, hospital housekeeping was chomping at the bit to clean my room for the next mama. He finally arrived, and we headed home as a family of three.

This little creature named Griffen rocked my world. Hard. As most moms can attest to, I wasn't prepared for life as a mom. He had a beautiful nursery, and his sleepers were neatly folded to prepare for his arrival. But that's about as much as I was prepared for. My little man cried day and night; he was inconsolable. I cried alongside him. Now I loved my son more than anything, but this wasn't just about love. I felt so much guilt when I wondered to myself, *What had I done? Maybe I wasn't cut out for this mom gig?* It felt so **hard**.

My husband struggled to help me. The moment he came home from work, I would head upstairs to lay down and rest. I was so tired and mentally fried, but I could not sleep through the frantic crying I would hear in the living room below. I felt that if Griffen was crying, I needed to be the one to hold him and try to *fix* it. This led me to visit multiple pediatricians who told me it was just a case of colic. I now know that colic is not an answer or a solution; it is a blanket statement that encompasses all fussy babies. "He will grow out of it," or "hang in there" were not helpful phrases and sent me further into an anxiety-ridden Google frenzy.

This was not my vision of motherhood. I had planned on long walks with my boy, showing him the world. Instead, I felt helpless and trapped. One day, we attempted a baby yoga class. Halfway through, the instructor gently suggested I try again next week when maybe the baby would be a bit more settled — quiet, she meant. I cried all the way home.

That night at three in the morning, I hit a breaking point. I asked my husband to pack my jeep; I was heading to my parents. This young mom needed hers. I showed up at their doorstep with my crying baby at five in the morning and crumbled. This was motherhood.

This went on for most of Griffen's first year. I still could not pinpoint what exactly was bothering him. He was growing and thriving but remained high maintenance. Everywhere I went, I took my yellow exercise ball to bounce on and soothe him. We wore the paint off that ball!

One day, when Griffen was eleven months old, I gave him a sip of cow's milk. He instantly could not breathe. I panicked, threw him in my jeep, and sped to the hospital. I bolted into emergency, with my baby in his Christmas jammies and full diaper, begging for help. They took him in and treated his allergic reaction and he was okay. I, however, was not. My husband met me at the hospital, and we left a few hours later with a referral to the allergist, an EpiPen, and a lot of anxiety.

I was returning to work and felt so scared that something would happen to him. That weekend, we went to a barbeque and I absolutely lost it when the host put cheese on the burgers in front of Griffen. None of the burgers were even for him! I was irrational and completely overwhelmed. On the plus side, we were finding answers for our boy and seeing his beautiful personality shine through as we finally figured out what was bothering his little system. My mom-guilt game was strong, and I was constantly beating myself up over not figuring everything out sooner. *I am a healthcare professional and couldn't even help my own boy.*

He grew. I calmed down. We adjusted. My marriage flourished as we finally found our groove with our baby. I was convinced I did not want more children, as the initial stages of motherhood had been really stressful for me.

Life felt great, perfect with one baby. He was our world. I worked permanent night shifts and gave all my spare time to being with my boy.

This went on for three years and eventually, my memories of Griffen's first year started to fade. We decided to have another baby, and four years after Griffen, we welcomed our second boy, Mikale.

I wanted someone to pinch me postpartum. This boy ate and slept on repeat. But I also carefully avoided all allergens, which meant he wasn't exposed to them and therefore not bothered. I felt so grateful for this boy and the chance to experience this piece of motherhood differently. Our family felt complete, and I felt confident managing my two little guys for the most part.

My boys grew and I carried on working shift work; nursing is a part of me. I felt so honored to support women through the birthing process. My husband and I did the juggle of work and small children like so many other families. He was always kind, supportive, and giving, and my children were happy and thriving. *So why did I feel so empty?*

At first, I pushed the feelings aside, ignoring the niggling thoughts in the back of my head. But they grew louder and louder until I could ignore them no longer. Maybe this was happening because we had started a family at quite a young age, and I hadn't seen the world yet. Maybe I wanted more from my career and contemplated medical school. But how would that look with a mortgage and two little boys?

My husband wondered what was wrong with me. On the surface, my life looked perfect; I wasn't unhappy with any one specific aspect, but knew I needed more. It was consuming me. I felt like I was performing half-assed in everything in my life. I was a mom, a wife, a nurse, a sister, and a friend, but I was not showing up for anything.

One night at midnight, my husband and I were sitting at our kitchen table. I was upset, as I had been for a few months. I couldn't figure out what my problem was. There was no reason for me to be unhappy. Sitting across from me was a supportive husband wanting to help; I had two beautiful little boys and a rewarding job. *What was my problem?* I felt like a shitty mom, a crappy wife, and a tired nurse. Reflecting back now, I think some would call it a "mid-life crisis," although I was only thirty-three years old. I felt antsy, anxious, and uncomfortable in my own skin.

Being the rock that he is, my husband listened without judgement. He offered insight that night. "Carrie, you have the kindest heart, you always have. I know your passion is nursing, that hasn't changed, but our world has! The definition of insanity is doing the same thing over and over and expecting a different result. We know for sure you need to nurse families to feel fulfilled. Why don't you do that, but start something that is yours?"

My husband has been an entrepreneur since the age of eighteen. We met when we were twenty, and the ironic thing is that I was always uninterested in business. I saw the hours and heart and soul he poured into his business and wasn't sure that route was for me. I loved nursing and leaving "work" at work to focus on my family. But like he said, that wasn't working for me anymore; I wasn't leaving it behind. In fact, I was dwelling on the fact I felt so unhappy. His words got my wheels turning. *What did private practice nursing look like? Could I find more time for myself that way? Would I feel better?* The tears stopped, and I told him I would think about it.

And so came The Mama Coach. Not overnight, but little by little, I built my own private practice business. I took my passion for serving others and built something on my own terms that left me fulfilled and lit a fire in me. I felt scared and sometimes ridiculous, as I did not have a business background. But I pushed past those feelings of vulnerability. I felt the uncertainty subside, and it was soon replaced with enthusiasm and a drive I didn't know I possessed. Entrepreneurship, something I had previously been annoyed by (the husband who missed endless family dinners and worked late hours), brought a welcome challenge into my life.

I quickly realized that mamas were looking for qualified support and education, without the judgment. Motherhood can be so tough, and I wanted to use my nursing skills to make it easier. There were programs out there trying to do that, but I wanted to take it a step further. I wrote my programming using evidence-informed research combined with a big dose of empathy. I was teaching prenatal classes, but not the traditional style class — I strived to make it comfortable and inclusive.

Although I am an IBCLC lactation consultant and am passionate about breastfeeding, I wanted my programs to be real and offer true support. I think it is unfair to teach that breastfeeding comes naturally to any woman and baby and is easy as a Sunday morning, as it takes practice from both mom and babe. Often the road of a breastfeeding journey is full of speed bumps and hard left turns. My programs reflected this and, as such, exploded.

And sleep. The basic need that gets overlooked and is the subject of jokes to young families everywhere. It is unfair to assume that because you have a child, you will never sleep again. But I also did not feel comfortable using some of the different "sleep training" methods out there. So instead, I wrote my own feeding-centered plans. They worked! Babies were feeding on demand and sleeping! My business kept growing exponentially — moms everywhere needed this safe space, community, and healing in order to further thrive in their lives as mothers, wives, humans. I was helping women enjoy motherhood and had never felt so amazing about my work and the new home life I was creating for myself.

It grew to the point of discomfort. I started a business to have more time for myself and my family but found myself consulting virtually across Canada seven days a week. Instead of getting upset over this dilemma, I realised the need for expansion. At that same kitchen table, I shared with Cody my plans to expand and build a licensing model that would allow registered nurses across Canada to be Mama Coaches and their own bosses. I wanted to give families everywhere the chance to have a face-to-face connection with a Mama Coach. I will never forget the look on his face when I told him that. As a seasoned entrepreneur, he knew how much work this would be. But he didn't discourage me and instead continued to be my biggest cheerleader.

I didn't wait long, mostly because I couldn't. I was busy and needed help. Through the help of a late-night Google search, I found a lawyer. We met a few days later and together, we built a licensing agreement, and I created an advertisement sharing my story and launched it on Facebook.

Twenty-four hours later, I woke up to sixty-five inquiries from registered nurses. They, too, wanted more time with their families and were feeling the burnout of shift work. I developed an application process. I did interview after interview and gradually built my team. Cody would return home from a week of work on Friday nights, and I would go to my Starbucks "office," only to basically return Sunday evening when he needed to leave again. I built guidebooks, templates, our website, and everything needed to expand successfully.

After one year of expansion, we are now a team of twenty-five nurses. Not only do I get to serve families, but I get to change the lives of the nurses who join our team as they build their own private practice. I have always said that one of the reasons I love nursing is because I love nurses! I consider them friends and am committed to mentoring each of them as they grow their business. We are creating a unique colleague relationship, as we are spread across the country yet so supportive of one another. We are busy working on new programming, and our vision is to become the one-stop shop of resources and support for parents from pregnancy into the teenage years. It has been beautiful to watch our business develop as each registered nurse has brought something unique to contribute. We are all nurses with different backgrounds and all mamas.

I often get asked about "my why." I can see the answer clearly now. Initially, it was because I felt uneasy and anxious about the life I was living, and I thought it was the answer to my problem. Now I know it is so much more than that. I have two little boys who watch everything I do, and all I want for them in their lives is one thing: happiness. As parents, we need to model the behavior we want to see in our children. How could I teach them to find joy in their life if I was unwilling to find joy in my own? I am modelling the joy I want them to feel in their lives. It isn't *perfect*, and I certainly don't have balance, but I feel content in our crazy life. And it shows. I am truly living my best life and feel so good knowing that my children are learning to value that most. My husband joined me full-time in The Mama Coach one year into our expansion, and we walk our kids to school together every morning. I get up early to work but find time for myself and my family every single day.

My boys are learning that they, too, can do challenging things — things that stretch them and provide growth! I am a registered nurse with zero business training, but I have built a company that is growing and providing for our family. They know and are proud of my story, and I get teary when I hear my sons talk about it. They are proud of me, and it feels so good.

Find joy in your world. If you aren't happy, there is a solution out there for you. Don't wait to look for it. Don't be scared to search for it and surround yourself with people who feel the same. You've got this, Mama!

~ To my sons. Griffen, my guinea pig when it comes to motherhood. Thank you for being so patient and loving while we figured you out. Mom loves you so much. And to my little guy, Mikale. You brighten each and every day with your bright and loving spirit. Lastly, my husband Cody. We met young and grew together. I am grateful every day to do life with you. Thank you for your endless support. I love you so much.

5

THE UNCONDITIONAL

by Cassie Jeans

"And so you wove me back together, You lit up my womb."

Cassie Jeans

Cassie Jeans is a #1 best-selling author, founder of the books series, *Her Art of Surrender* and a dedicated leader for women who want to fully embrace all aspects of their soul and take full ownership of their life. She is an advocate for the transformational power self-worth has in a woman's life and has a gift of eradicating self-doubt and limiting beliefs using the power of words, practical step-by-step solutions, and the wisdom of intuition. She is interested in what lights up a person's soul and guides them to see that by following that path alone — all other core desires will naturally fall into place.

She is the creator of *In The Bedroom w/ Cassie Jeans: Words That Awaken The Soul* podcast. This podcast is lit and divine and embodies so much of who she is and is receiving rave reviews internationally. Another great place to hang out with Cassie is her Instagram account, which is like her public journal and is filled with poems, beautiful pictures, and life tips for those who dream of something more.

www.cassiejeans.com
ig: @cassie_mjeans
fb: @cassiemjeans

When I held you in my arms, I had all the feels.
I felt love for you,
I felt the overwhelm of this love,
The unconditional,
All-encompassing love that everyone talked about.
That I dreamed about,
That I knew I would feel.
What I did not know was the anguish that accompanied the love.
The fear,
The desperation,
The loneliness . . .
Oh the loneliness was the worst.
Where did I go as I held you in my arms?
Why was the dark accompanied by what was,
At the time,
The most perfect love?
And so, I spiraled down the hole
Longing to land somewhere that made sense
But finding myself,
Displaced,
Cut open,
Not-whole.

~ Cassie Jeans

~ To: Elijah, Calista, Joel,
Mom, Dad, Ray, Latara, Dan, Cindy,
the tribe that helps my children grow.

W hat was I to do? Postpartum depression (PPD) hit me like a ton of bricks, and I had no idea what was going on. All I knew is that the feeling was one of overwhelming loneliness. If I'm being honest, this period of my life still shakes me up when I think of it. The thoughts running through my mind scared me. I was too afraid to share what I was really feeling. Years worth of learning how to stuff down my emotions and keep them neatly tucked away created an internal storm of agony.

Photos from this time show otherwise, and I am grateful they are there because I know I was happy amidst the feelings of isolation. I knew the love for my kids was real, yet I can remember the two conflicting conversations in my head. *Cassie, this will be okay. Cassie, sleep will come. Cassie, they grow up so fast, enjoy this time. Cassie, why aren't you enjoying this? Cassie, what's wrong with you?*

There was this pressure building up within me to do it all right. All of it. I made it my mission to bring the healthiest, most emotionally secure, most loved children into the world, and I did endless research to ensure that I would do it the "right" way. I remember ordering books online, reading, making my husband read, asking tons of questions of my midwives to make sure they had the answers I was looking for, all in an attempt to control the experience. I wanted to get this right so badly that I forgot to enjoy it. All that mattered to me was that *I* would be their mother and they would be *my* children.

And *that* right there was where things would come undone. This idea that somehow they were mine. That because I birthed them, I had a right to ownership, which would put me in the driver's seat and make me responsible for their entire life. I was the teacher, the guardian, the everything. The truth, however, which I came to understand after postpartum depression had balanced and I had done (and still continue to do) years of personal development and spiritual growth, was this: I do not own my children. They are their own. I am not responsible for the entirety of their life. I am a guide.

And even more than this, they are my greatest teachers. They are my guide in this life, and this agreement is sacred and divinely orchestrated for the growth of us all as individuals. We are connected, yet apart. We are intertwined, yet sovereign.

What would happen if we allowed our children the courtesy of being seen as the wise teachers they are? What would happen if we asked them to formulate their own ideas instead of projecting ours onto them? What would happen if we let them feel their emotions outright instead of forcing them to bottle them up to fit into whatever expectation we have about being emotional? I believe they would rise to the occasion and that whatever lessons learned along the way would serve not only their life path but ours as moms and dads, too.

Mom, pay attention to your emotions. I had no idea how wound up I was emotionally until the epic adventure of motherhood began. Everyone around me seemed to have the child-rearing thing down to a science, so I tried to find myself in that modality of life, too. I am woman, women have children, children complete woman, this is fulfillment.

Only I couldn't connect to this at all. I would always come back to this idea that there was something wrong with me, but as it turns out, I was asking the wrong question. The real question underneath it all was, "Why do I feel this way?" There is always a reason for our feelings, and the longer I pushed the emotions away, the worse I became as a mom.

Lao Tzu says, "When the student is ready, the teacher will appear." What this quote doesn't do is give a standard or a checklist for what a *teacher* actually means. The children I birthed came into my life to teach me how to be a better person. I wasn't living my best life before them. They disrupted my whole path — and I say that with a lot of joy because without the disruption, I wouldn't be who I am today. So far, they have taught me to be more observant of my reactions. To own my feelings. To release my control. To find myself. To love myself.

Anger was the first emotion we would tackle together. As is most often the case, this was a bumpy road. I was completely unaware of how angry an adult I was. Children amplified that anger in ways I never thought possible. I own this now, but there were times when I was mean. I remember when my son was so young and we were rushing out the door. Anxiety mounted inside me every time we were in a rush, which was pretty well every morning. It was a cool day and they needed mittens. My youngest was bundled in her car seat, which she hated, and I knew we were in for a car ride of screaming and crying. I had handed my two-year-old son a pair of slip-on gloves — only these ones were not *slipping on* at all. I remember yelling so severely at him for not being able to get his fingers in each hole. I think I even used the words, "What's wrong with you? Why can't you get these on?"

But what I was really saying was, "What's wrong with me? Why can't I be a better mom?!" I'll never forget his little fingers desperately trying to get in the holes, trying not to make mommy mad, the look on his face, the desire to please me even when I was being a total jerk. This was a really low moment, one that haunts me. This was the "Something has got to change and it's got to change now. Mommy, this isn't how you talk to me" moment.

And thankfully, I did. I started taking care of my physical, mental, and emotional self, using help from health practitioners and personal growth coaches. I knew my responses were not acceptable and I didn't want to keep acting as if they were. One of the most beautiful gifts emerged from having to face my emotions. I knew I wanted to raise children who didn't have to be afraid of their mom, and because I believed I could do better and because I practiced real, soul-shaking self-love, I was given the gift of grace and forgiveness. My children blanketed me in grace and through this, I learned to say sorry.

"I'm sorry. Mommy shouldn't have yelled like that. I'm sorry, that was not nice of me."

Such an incredible gift. Because I was willing to pick up the mirror and stare back at the woman who was not giving motherhood her best, I was gifted the opportunity to change the reflection. There were two little beings in my life who loved me unconditionally and never gave up on who they knew I was deep down inside. They never had to say, "Mom, you can do better." They just loved me and accepted me every step of the way. I can never thank them enough for being the reflection I needed the most at that time.

As we healed our way through anger, the doors opened up for communication and patience. Communication is a two-way street. Just because I am the adult, that does not mean I get to speak, have the last word, or be right. I needed to listen to my children and slow down my own thoughts to fully engage with their ideas, emotions, wonderings, questions, insights, frustrations; basically every thought they had going through their brain was valid. I did not need to run over their processing just because I had the answer. I learned to hold space for their inquiring minds and growing curiosities. I learned to slow down when topics would come up that might have made me uncomfortable and to allow for the answers or the "I don't knows" to be shared in the space of communication. Patience went hand-in-hand with communication.

Slow down, Mom, you're going too fast. The art of listening, the art of stillness, the art of the quieted mind. As moms, it is true, we have a whirling catalogue of information going through our minds pretty well every second of the day. But our children, they live in the moment, in the now. When I would stop, breathe, and focus on them completely, I was led into the stillness with them. I was led into the wonder of the world, the fascination of discovery, the sensation of taking it all in. This agreement, of student-teacher, teacher-student, was opening up a world within me that had been locked away for so long. I remembered my childhood through watching them explore theirs. This was another gift that they offered by simply being.

Mom, we don't need you to have it all together, we need you whole. And in this realization, the shackles of perfection crumbled off. These boulders of shame and of caring about what others thought finally rolled off of my shoulders and shattered all around me. I gave myself permission to find what truly lit me up. I was viewing the way I was raising my children through too many lenses that as an individual, separate from my children, I did not align with. I was trying to be all the things I was seeing in other people, and the exhaustion from trying to keep up with it all overwhelmed my ability to lean into my intuition.

What did I want my children to remember me for? What was the legacy I would leave behind? Would they be okay if I truly lived to the beat of my own drum? Could I do that and still be a fully engaged mom? The truth that I found for myself was, yes. When I light up and give up the life of the "sacrificial-mom," my children instinctively tapped into what lit them up, too.

With every success I shared with them about how my week went or what had happened in my business or what had gone wrong, they would lean in, listen, ask questions, and cheer me on. We were building a symbiotic relationship in which I share with them my thoughts, emotions, and wonderings and they share with me their opinions, their desires . . . their dreams.

> "No greater gift, than to plant the seed of wonder. No greater delight, than to nourish the dreams of the young, the wild, the unfettered."
> ~ Cassie Jeans

I make no claim on their life. I only promise to love them unconditionally, to be open to receiving them as they come to me, and to allow them to teach me about who I want to be in the world. There is a togetherness, this energetic cord that bonds us with our children. When we allow for flexibility in this union and let go of our story about how it is all supposed to come together, we open ourselves to the gift of learning from one another about how to experience our humanity in so many beautiful ways.

> And so you wove me back together,
> You lit up my womb,
> the darkest part of my body,
> You brought life into.
> You were the seed of life that my soul craved,
> The awakening of my spirit,
> The dawn of my journey home.

> ~Sealed with light, by Cassie Jeans

Wherever you are right now in the journey of motherhood, there are a few questions I can offer as a guide. I am still learning, still growing, still embodying this message deeper into my heart and soul. It is easy to hold onto what we wish we didn't do as moms, but this does not serve us at all. In the moments when life is overwhelming and frustration creeps in, ask yourself these questions:

What is the kindest thing I can do for myself right now? This question is so vital. The automatic response is usually of shame, guilt, and anger and is not in alignment with self-love. Practicing self-kindness is a vital first step.

Everything we do as moms, our children are observing. This isn't meant to sound terrifying because remember, they have a responsibility in their journey to own their story, the same way we do. Rather, view it as a gift. When you choose self-kindness, they observe the results of that choice.

What do I *not* need to do right now? This is when we slow down as moms. Slowing down allows you to catch your breath and realign. Do you need to lie down for twenty minutes instead of folding the laundry? It is okay if the laundry stays in the basket and doesn't get folded until tomorrow. What are you prioritizing ahead of your own self-care? Remember, as a mom, you are still allowed to be an important person in the room.

Why do I feel this way? Always ask why questions when it comes to your emotions. Overwhelm is a common emotion for many moms, but why? Are you taking on too much? Are you expecting too much of yourself? Are you sad, lonely, scared? If life is feeling intense and you are worried at all, talk to a friend, a counselor, a coach, a health practitioner. Personally, I advocate first for holistic treatments that don't cover up the emotions associated with motherhood. These can include homeopathy, nutritional cleansing, meditation, prayer, and spiritual guidance.

Who can I call for help? There is always someone in your corner. Right now, you are holding a book written by moms who are journeying this experience alongside you. Tap into the resources that are available to you and choose to do something about your own story. Helpers are everywhere. I know that sharing how you really feel takes a great deal of courage, but it is necessary so you don't hold what you are feeling in and stay silent. You have every right to ask for help.

How do I want my children to feel today in my presence? I leave this question until the end for a very specific reason. Ask yourself this only after you have gone through the first four questions. You matter. You are important. Learn to self-reflect so that you can be intentional about what you want to reflect to your kiddos. The only way to do this is to take the time to be with yourself and to learn to love your whole self in the most beautiful way.

Sending an abundance of love.

Section 2
EVEN MIRACLES AREN'T *PERFECT*

FEATURING

Aimee Swift

Jessica Sharpe

Jessica Lance

Tia Slightham

Lisa Mechor

OPENING COMMENTARY BY

Sabrina Greer

*N*ot everyone knows this about me, but a massive part of my undergraduate psychology studies was in cognitive behavior, disability studies, and brain development. After adopting my siblings, all of whom have special needs, I felt more inclined to participate in this research and to arm myself with knowledge and awareness to advocate for the people who needed a louder voice. I volunteered at the Geneva Centre for Autism and took my post-grad Behavioral Intervener Certification course through them. Having a brother with high functioning autism and watching him overcome challenges inspired this decision. I also worked at an integrative preschool that was for predominantly special needs children. This was inspired by my adopted sister, who has Fetal Alcohol Syndrome (FAS) and to this day, in her thirties, lives with my senior parents.

I have a lot of experience with many levels of physical and emotional challenges and cognitive delays, but like all parents, I hope and pray my children are what *they* call "typically developing." I say this as my toddler is pulling a thread on his pants, resembling a dog chasing his tail. I feel incredibly blessed that we weren't given additional challenges. Parenting is already so hard. Motherhood is already so hard.

But as I mentioned in the introduction, it is not about comparing whose journey is harder or more challenging than others'. I am incredibly grateful that my children are healthy and developing "typically." I hope as you read the following section, instead of feeling sorry for the brave souls sharing their stories, you view these warrior women and their precious little gems through a lens of nothing but mad respect.

Yes, their children have been giving heftier obstacles, which in turn adds additional challenges for these mamas. But their courage and strength is sure to inspire you and make you squeeze your babes a little harder. Once we move past surrendering to the concept of perfect timing, we can move to another important ideology — acceptance. Sometimes it is hard to accept our fate when it is less than perfect. I love this quote from Amy Tam: *"If you can't change your fate, change your attitude."* I think you will see this concept expressed throughout this section.

6

JOY IN THE UNEXPECTED

by Aimee Swift

"Life may be different, but it will be so beautiful."

Aimee Swift

Aimee Swift is a mama to two beautiful girls, Eliza Rose and Lindie Fern, and is married to her college sweetheart, Chris. The four of them live in Tulsa, Oklahoma. A lover of flowers and coffee, Aimee was born and raised in Missouri. There she pursued a bachelor's degree in Biology and a master's degree in Science Education at the University of Missouri. She spent four years working as a middle school teacher before she followed her dream to be a stay-at-home mama. Aimee became a Down syndrome advocate the day her youngest daughter, Lindie, was born with an unexpected Down syndrome diagnosis. She loves educating herself and others about the beauty that can be found in a Down syndrome diagnosis, all while vulnerably shedding light on the challenges that come with raising a child with special needs. An eternal optimist and cheerleader for the underdog, Aimee spends her days hopping between doctors' appointments, library story times, and splash pad playdates. She loves to read, decorate her home with DIY crafts, and pursue her relationship with Jesus. She hopes to write her own book and dreams of living in the country. Armed with dry shampoo and all things floral, Aimee loves seeking joy in the everyday and sharing all about it on her blog.

www.aimeebeeblog.com
ig: @aimeeswift

Photographer credit: Cassy Pack Photography

*"Life is what happens to you while you're
busy making other plans."*
~ John Lennon

I awoke to the sound of my dad's voice.

"Wake up."

My dad had passed away two years before from cancer. It was one of those things that was so sudden. One day he was at my daughter's birthday party, and the next he was told he had terminal cancer. He died two months after his diagnosis. It was enough time to say what we needed to say, but not enough time at all. I dreamed about him often. Some nights we would carry on as if nothing had happened. Other nights he would tell me things I needed to hear. On the day Lindie was born, he told me to wake up.

It was 2:30am when I awoke. I was having contractions. I got out of bed and went to the bathroom.

My pregnancy with Lindie was so much like my pregnancy with Eliza, my eldest daughter. I was sick through the whole first trimester. All I craved was meat, McDonald's breakfast sandwiches, and cold vegetable soup from a can. I never threw up but always felt like I needed to. Coffee, which I lived on before I was pregnant, made me sick, and the smell of popcorn made me cringe.

Back on the toilet, I questioned if I was actually in labor. My contractions weren't very painful, but they weren't going away either. I left the bathroom and nudged my sleeping husband. "I think I'm having contractions," I told him. "I'm going to the living room to time them."

No response. He's hard to wake sometimes.

I went to the living room, got on all fours, and I timed each contraction as I went through the laboring techniques we had discussed with my doula. Thirty minutes had passed when I heard Eliza's steps. She walks just like me. A petite little frame but the stomp of an elephant.

"What are you doing, Mama?"

Chris awoke when Eliza did and came into the living room. It was now past 3am and my contractions were consistently less than five minutes apart. He made the arrangements we had been talking about for months. First, he called our doula to let her know I was in labor. Next, he called my mom and told her it was time. Then he called our friends who had agreed to watch Eliza. Before Eliza left, I hugged her hard. I was so mixed with emotions. I knew it was the last time it would be just the two of us and that brought me to tears. At the same time, I was so excited to meet Lindie. I kissed Eliza goodbye and continued to labor.

Time went on in a blur. My doula arrived. The contractions became closer together and more painful. I labored in a ton of different positions. Wanting to labor naturally, I chose to stay home as long as possible with both my girls to avoid any unnecessary interventions at the hospital. I labored leaning on Chris, on hands and knees in the tub, and on the toilet. We even took a walk down the street early in the morning. I remember walking back to the house, watching the sunrise in the middle of the contractions and thinking, "Today Lindie will see this sun!"

After sunrise, things progressed rather quickly. We loaded up the car and headed to the hospital. Once we arrived, they wheeled me into a room and determined I was dilated seven centimeters. I was so happy but had no time to show it. The contractions were unbearable. I questioned my decision to forgo the epidural. Too late for that. It was go time!

I continued to labor while the nurses scrambled to get everything ready and locate my doctor. After several more contractions, I had the intense urge to push. I told the nurses, but they told me to wait a little longer. It took everything in me not to push, and I said, "I think she's coming!"

They turned me over only to see Lindie's head crowning. Within seconds, my doctor was there in gown and told me to push. I pushed three times during the length of one contraction and after the third push, at 8:54am on Saturday, March 4, 2017, after only six and a half hours of labor, she came flying out into the world, sac and all! She landed in my doctor's hands and the sac burst, covering my doctor and the floor below her in amniotic fluid. And then there she was!

And then there she was!

Immediately, they put her in my arms. I held her and couldn't believe she was here; she was mine, and we were meeting for the first time. Even though she was my second, it felt awkward holding such a tiny frame all over again.

Right away, the nurses took her from me because "her color was off" and they suspected "she swallowed fluid." Lindie hadn't cried yet. They took her to the incubator and rubbed her body and sucked her mouth and stomach. She was only a few feet away in that tiny incubator, but it might as well have been miles. I wanted to reach out and grab her. My placenta was passing, but my eyes were fixed on her. I watched everything they did.

After the placenta passed, they brought her back to my chest and continued sucking her throat and stomach. I took her in. She was covered in a thick layer of vernix with dark hair, and she was mine. I still couldn't believe she was real, and I couldn't believe she was mine!

My doctor finished up and said her goodbyes. Chris was standing to my right holding me, holding Lindie. Together, we were staring at this beauty that was ours, the beauty we had dreamed about for so many months. This was the little Lindie Fern we had talked about before she was even conceived. This was the little Lindie Fern for whom we had hung cloud mobiles from the ceiling and then rehung them another time after Eliza got too rowdy with her friend and pulled them down. This was the little Lindie Fern I had predicted would be a genius because of the crazy logic puzzle addiction I had while she was in the womb. This was the Lindie Fern who had caused us to travel up and down the attic in search of the tiny baby clothes settling there in the totes and dust, having to wash, fold, sort, and organize in time for her arrival. This was the little Lindie Fern our friends had showered with beautiful baby clothes, books, and the kindest gifts. This was the little Lindie

Fern whom we prayed for, asked God for, and trusted his provision for. And she was here!

And this was it: the dividing line. The line between the time when we thought everything was as it seemed and little Lindie Fern was who we thought she was and the moment we realized she, in fact, was not.

In that same moment, while Chris was to my right holding me, holding Lindie, and we were soaking her in, a nurse walked up to us to my left and said, "I want to be upfront with you. Your daughter shows characteristics of having Down syndrome." And then she showed us the three characteristics: the fold on the back of her neck, her lower set ears, and the palmar crease on her hands. Then she asked, "Do you have any questions?"

We stared at each other, our expressions blank, our hearts in shock. There were no words to be said because who the heck has words to say in that moment? We hadn't even begun processing this news when she walked away. No explanations or compassion. Just protocol.

In *that* moment, everything changed.

This is the part I wish I could go back in time and do myself. I wish I could have been the one to deliver the news. I wish I could have been the one to tell the two of us caught-off-guard thirty-year-old parents that it would be okay. I wish I could deliver the news of Down syndrome with hope, compassion, tenderness, and encouragement. I wish I could have said, "Things will be different. Things may be hard. But it will be okay. She's your daughter. She's loved and she's beautiful. There are beautiful things ahead, even with a Down syndrome diagnosis!"

Instead the news was delivered by a textbook, and then the textbook walked away.

My mom arrived shortly after. The timing. I couldn't even open my mouth to speak the words "Down syndrome." They sounded so harsh and ugly and foreign mulling around my mouth. *Down syndrome. How could those words possibly describe the baby who had been in my body for nine months?* Somehow I mustered up the words.

"They think she has Down syndrome," I told her.

My mom immediately said something positive, but I wasn't ready for that. I wanted to go back to the fifteen minutes before, or was it thirty minutes or an hour? I wanted to go back before the darn dividing line! I wanted her to be "normal" and healthy and I wanted excitement to fill the room! For God's sake, I wanted a do-over! In life, we are given so many do-overs, and this was the time I wanted mine!

But instead, I stared at this little girl like I didn't know her. And I didn't. I had no idea what her diagnosis meant. I barely knew anyone with Down syndrome, let alone my flesh and blood who grew inside my body for nine months. How could I not have known? She was my flesh and blood, but she didn't feel like it. So there I was holding this child I didn't know or understand, with nothing to say, and I kept wondering when the baby I had expected would be born.

The next few days followed in a blur. They were dark and full of tears. They were thick with grief and tainted with those difficult words: Down syndrome.

We were transferred to postpartum. Our family and close friends knew she had arrived, but they didn't know the news. We couldn't even find the words to say anything to each other, how could we find the words to tell everyone else? I remember at one point asking Chris to pray that the doctors and nurses were wrong, to pray that it wasn't true or if it was that God would reverse it — every single tiny microscopic cell, every single one, so that the diagnosis would be reversed. I believe God has the power to do anything He wants and, at the time, I wanted so badly for this to be wrong. I wanted this to be a bad dream from which we would soon be woken up.

Chris' parents were on their way, so I asked him to tell them the news before they arrived. I couldn't bear the thought of seeing their responses in person. I wanted everyone to know before they came to me so that I didn't have to bear the weight of seeing their reactions replay in my mind for eternity. He reluctantly agreed. I did the same with my mom, asking her to tell my siblings and then asking them to pass the news to our extended family.

I held Lindie and saw sadness. I laid her in her bassinet and saw sadness. I tried to nurse her and saw sadness. I started pumping and continued to try to nurse her and saw sadness. I saw family hold her and love on her and stare at her, yet all I saw was sadness. My whole body, from head to toe, was covered in sadness. Every single one of my tiny microscopic cells, every single one.

And yet, amid it all, I felt a sliver of hope. I was reminded that even though we may have been surprised by her diagnosis, God was not one bit surprised and valued her just as she was — little Lindie Fern, our beautiful daughter with Down syndrome.

The first afternoon of Lindie's life, Eliza arrived and my heart broke all over again. About a month before Lindie was born, I took Eliza to pick out a "welcome gift" for her. After forty-five minutes of scouring the aisles, Eliza picked out a beautiful pink owl rattle with bright geometric patterns. The present sat on our entryway table for weeks as a bright reminder of the gift that was coming our way.

When Eliza walked in the hospital room that afternoon, gift in hand, my heart sank. It was a reminder of the life we used to have. The simple life. All along, I thought Lindie would simply fit into our way of life, but now everything had changed. The dividing line. Everything was so much different from what I had expected, and I didn't get the chance to warn her.

But if my heart was breaking, Eliza didn't notice. She walked into the room, shy yet excited to meet her baby sister. She hopped up on the hospital bed, gave me a hug, and stared at her sister with true love. Her baby sister was here, and she couldn't help but smile out of sheer joy! Seeing the two of them together, Eliza's excitement and unconditional love for Lindie, gave me another sliver of hope when I so desperately needed it.

Lindie's struggle to breathe at the start of her life was a sign of things to come. Before we even left the hospital, Lindie had her first echocardio-gram and within twenty-four hours of going home, we returned via the emer-gency room. That night she had a chest x-ray, an abdominal x-ray, a pelvic ultrasound, an abdominal ultrasound, and a list of blood tests too long to mention. I remember watching her little body lying limp on the bed in the emergency room. She was so tiny on the giant bed, surrounded by beeping machines and already hooked up to too many cords. I remember looking at Chris and asking him, "How did we get here? How is this our real life?" Here I was, four days postpartum, still bleeding from my bottom and breast pump-ing in the nurse's station, when I should have been at home happily cuddling and breastfeeding my newborn baby.

Lindie spent thirty-five days in the Neonatal Intensive Care Unit (NICU). She had two surgeries and weeks of recovery. But finally, we were discharged from the hospital and brought her home.

Bringing her home was so incredible! We were elated to be together, all four of us. We were eager to establish a routine and loved having her in our arms while we watched movies on the couch or on the floor while playing with Eliza. It was so simple, yet it felt so complete!

At the same time, bringing Lindie home was also a dismal realization. It was a slap back to reality. Because things were so urgent and scary in the NICU, we hadn't spent a lot of time processing her diagnosis. Leaving the NICU and bringing her home was the beginning of our journey to acceptance — to making our peace with the hand the Lord had dealt. I wish I could say that the making peace part happened quickly for me, but it didn't. For the first three months of Lindie's life, every time I looked at her, I saw Down syndrome. I was so sensitive and insecure about it all. I was worried about what people would say at doctor's appointments and Chick-Fil-A. I avoided taking pictures of her from certain angles that made her look like she had Down syndrome. I would compare her to the other babies around us or on social media. I didn't go a day, or some days even an hour, without thinking about Down syndrome.

It wasn't until the end of May that things changed. One day while Eliza was napping, I took Lindie out on the porch swing. I remember sitting on the swing, holding her in my arms and staring into her eyes, when it finally clicked. I loved her. Just her. Not her without Down syndrome or her in the pictures when she looked "normal" or her on days without a million doctors' appointments. I loved her. Period.

That day was a new dividing line. It wasn't a line that marked the end of my grief and processing or difficult days, but it was a line that marked the way my eyes saw Lindie. For the first time, I saw her and loved her completely, not despite Down syndrome, but Down syndrome and all.

Slowly but surely things changed, in my heart and in my head. I became so attached and fell overwhelmingly in love with my daughter, just as I had with Eliza when she was born, that I didn't want her to be any different than who she was. My whole body was covered in love for her, every one of my cells, regardless of how many chromosomes were in hers. And as my love for her grew, my insecurities and fears lessened. The days got easier.

Growing up, my dad was known for his "Dad-isms." He would say things like, "Can a jar be ajar?" or "One hundred years — all new people!" Sometimes he referenced famous quotes or songs. One of his favorites that he would often share with me was from the late John Lennon: *"Life is what happens to you while you're busy making other plans."* When things in my life were not going the way I planned or when challenges came my way, he would often remind me of this. It became such a sweet reminder that I even painted the words on a canvas shortly after he passed away.

Lindie's birth diagnosis of Down syndrome was unexpected. Everything was so shocking. The news was traumatic to my core. It was traumatic to my plans. All along, I had envisioned bringing a second child into the world who would fit the mold of our family. Instead she shattered that mold. And yet, instead of that mold remaining shattered, Lindie's life forced us to rise again and create a new family mold. Something even more beautiful than before. One that is inclusive. One that fights for justice. One full of joy, and one that always exudes love and says, "You matter." One that says, "Life may be different, but it will be so beautiful."

> ~ To Eliza Rose — for making me a mama and
> loving unconditionally. To Lindie Fern — our
> greatest surprise who challenges us to love bigger.
> To Chris — my faithful best friend, and to my own
> parents — my Mom who is my greatest cheerleader
> and my Dad, whose words are still life-changing.

7

COMING HOME

by *Jessica Sharpe*

"A positive mindset has the power to create miracles."

Jessica Sharpe

Jessica is a serial entrepreneur who knew from a young age she was destined for a big life. She left home at seventeen years old and moved to Toronto, where she pursued her studies in advertising. She began her career as an advertising sales executive at a luxury lifestyle publication, followed by a move to two out-of-home media companies. It was here that she met the man she knew would be her husband. Leaving the world of advertising behind, Jessica opened the doors to her first brick-and-mortar business at twenty-four, a boutique tanning studio and swimwear shop in downtown Toronto. She's often described as driven and fiercely determined and is someone who loves change. It was after the birth of her second daughter that she started her next business venture and forever-career with a global network marketing company, Arbonne International. Jessica is passionate about fitness, fashion, plant-based food, and inspiring and empowering others to dream big and live their best life. Arbonne is her vehicle to live a life by design and practice healthy living on a daily basis while teaching others how to do the same. She spends her days splitting time between business and her two girls, Abigail (age four) and Isla (age two), while making a conscious effort to hit the gym regularly and do the things that make her happy, knowing she is a better mom, wife, and boss because of it.

www.JessSharpe.arbonne.com | www.luxetanning.ca
ig: @JessicaSharpe__

"Staying positive doesn't mean you have to be happy all the time. It means that even on hard days you know that there are better ones coming."
~ Unknown

A pediatrician waited in the delivery room for my daughter's arrival — a common protocol since it was a week past her due date and there could be meconium in her lungs that would need to be cleared. The midwives warned me of this, in case she didn't cry right away like you see in the movies. I was feeling renewed energy, knowing I would hold my baby for the first time in just a matter of minutes, but I could never have prepared for what happened next.

I had a great pregnancy. Sure, I was nauseous most days for the first couple months, but once I was a few weeks into my second trimester, I felt amazing! In fact, there were days I would've sworn I wasn't pregnant if it hadn't been for my growing belly. I hit the gym three times a week, stayed busy running my businesses, and took advantage of the flexibility I had in my schedule to design our baby's nursery and shop for crib sheets and adorable outfits.

My husband and I always joke that we never have a period of time when we're *settled*. There's always something massive happening in our lives keeping us in a perpetual state of chaos, and this time was no different. We were living through a home renovation, and I was in the midst of closing one of my businesses so I could spend more time with our newborn. Our home renovations wrapped up just before our baby was born, as did my negotiations with my business subtenant. Although we were closing in on my due date, everything was going according to plan.

Speaking of plans, I had chosen to go the midwife route with this pregnancy and felt very comfortable with my choice to have a hospital birth. I remember my first visit to the midwives' clinic and being asked how I felt about pain management during labour. I explained that since this is my first baby, I have no idea how I'm going to feel, but my intention is to see how things go naturally and then decide. I was absolutely open to having an epidural if I should want one when the time came, and I was happy to hear this wouldn't be a problem with the midwives — they would simply transfer care to the hospital team and reappear to care for the baby when she arrived.

At thirty-nine weeks pregnant, my feet and ankles, which my sister lovingly called "cankles," started to swell, thus ending my annoyingly perfect pregnancy. Forty weeks came and went, and I was trying to naturally induce labour in any way I could — from acupuncture to spending hours walking around several different shopping malls, I did it all. I woke up with excruciating back pain for a few nights in a row, and at forty-one weeks, I was finally in labour.

Back labour. I recalled reading about this and from what I knew, it meant the baby was facing the wrong way (face-up instead of down), which causes a ton of pressure. Read: pain. Every contraction took my breath away, and everything I learned in my prenatal classes went out the window. I've always had a high pain tolerance, but this was in a league of its own. The midwives came to my house to check on me and concluded that I would continue to labour at home. Twelve excruciating hours later, after many showers and baths and failed attempts to nap, my water broke in our bedroom. It caught me off guard, and I let out a shriek as I noticed right away that the pool on the floor was brown. I remembered hearing somewhere that this was meconium, "baby's first poo," and can happen if the baby is past their due date. After a quick call to the midwives, off to the hospital we went.

After my water broke, the pain became even more unbearable and I asked my midwife for an epidural as soon as we arrived at the hospital. She brushed the request off and said I should wait it out for a while. I didn't question her. Hours passed, and things weren't progressing as quickly as I expected. The baby still wasn't facing the right way, so the midwife had me push to get my baby in position. I asked multiple times over the next few hours about the status of my epidural, to no avail.

I have always been a strong-willed person and although I can be soft-spoken, I am not afraid to my voice my opinions. During my birth experience, however, the pain and feeling of complete overwhelm took over and I put my trust in the professionals. After all, this was my first baby. My wonderful, calm, and supportive husband was beside me the entire time, but he didn't advocate for me. To this day, he doesn't know and can't explain why he didn't speak up, except that he trusted that the midwife team had my best interest at heart.

After over five hours of pushing, which I later found out is not normal, I begged the midwife to give me something for the pain. She said I could have a shot of morphine to help me rest. I was desperate for some relief and agreed to the morphine shot. The morphine did nothing for the pain and just made me feel drugged and groggy.

It was six hours of pushing before my baby girl arrived. I felt physically exhausted, had burst a blood vessel in my eye from pushing so hard, and my legs were numb — but not from an epidural, as I never got one. Somehow in my twelve hours of laboring at the hospital, I did not have the right to an epidural. *This*, I will never understand.

We welcomed our baby girl into the world on March 28, 2015 at 5:07am. She wasn't breathing. The pediatrician and team whisked her away to clear her lungs, but something else was wrong. I was so out of it from the morphine shot, but I could tell by the look on my husband's face that it wasn't good. The hospital team took over for the midwives, and I sensed that they were trying desperately to save my minutes-old baby. I remember the pediatrician rushing over to my bedside, holding my baby out as if to hand her over, and I reached out my arms, eager to see her face and hold her for the first time. But he said, "I have to take her now" and disappeared.

We were living any parents' worst nightmare. In that moment, I knew we needed to give our precious baby a name. We had a short list of a few names, but my husband and I both called out Abigail. Her middle name would be

Grace. My husband was reluctant to leave my side, but I instructed him to go to our daughter. I needed him to be with her more than I needed him beside me. I regretted the morphine shot with my whole being. I was alone, helpless, and scared. An overwhelming feeling of emptiness consumed me. My husband was racing back and forth from the hospital's Neonatal Intensive Care Unit (NICU) to my bedside, and I kept asking him if our baby was okay. With tears in his eyes, he told me he didn't know and that it was her brain. The doctors informed us that Abigail would be taken to Sick Kids Hospital, where she would undergo therapeutic hypothermia to stop her brain from swelling any further.

The second time I saw my baby girl was in an incubator on a stretcher, when the nurses from the Sick Kids transport team brought her to see me before she left in an ambulance. I asked if I could touch her through the tiny hole in the plastic, and they said of course I could.

It had only been two hours since Abigail was born, and I was ready to be discharged from the hospital. Since I didn't have an epidural and was under midwife care, there was no reason for them to keep me there any longer. I hadn't slept for twenty-eight hours and was in a state of shock. My parents offered to go with Abigail to Sick Kids Hospital so that she wouldn't be alone and so my husband and I could take a nap at home before joining them.

We slept for a couple of hours and I woke up hoping everything that had happened was just a bad dream. But I was no longer pregnant; I was empty. No baby in my now-deflated belly and no baby on my chest.

We drove to Sick Kids Hospital, where my dad was waiting for us with a wheelchair for me. He showed us to the room where Abigail was staying in the NICU. The words on the door turned my stomach to knots and my heart raced as we approached the nursing desk. With a genuine smile on her face, the first thing the nurse said to us was, "Congratulations." I couldn't bring myself to respond.

There she was, lying on her back with wires attached to her chest and head, a breathing tube up her tiny nose, and a feeding tube with a little heart-shaped bandage adhered to her cheek. Her precious body was kept alive only by these big, beeping machines. Upon closer look, I noticed that they had to shave some of her hair so they could attach probes to her head to monitor her brain activity. She also had a large, red bruise on her head, which they later told me was from all the pushing. I cried then for the first time since she had been born that morning, seeing firsthand the magnitude of what had happened.

We were told that we could stay at her bedside as much as we wanted and while we couldn't hold her, we could touch her, talk to her, sing to her, and read to her. It had only been six hours since I gave birth to my baby, but I felt I had no time for my wheelchair. I knew I was weak, but I wanted to see my baby, I needed to stand at her bedside close enough to her face so that she could feel my breath on her cheek and hear my words in her ear. I told her that I loved her for the first time and that I couldn't wait to take her home.

Abigail underwent a therapeutic hypothermia treatment for seventy-two hours; after she warmed up again, she was sent for an MRI to assess the damage to her brain. We met with a neurologist who told us that during the long delivery and extensive pushing phase, the oxygen to her brain was cut off. That would explain why she still wasn't breathing on her own and showed no signs of reflexes. Her brain wasn't telling her body to do these things.

After our first of many long days and nights at the hospital, we went home to sleep. The NICU nursing team would take care of Abigail during the night and we could call at any point for updates. And so our routine began. My husband and I woke up every three hours so I could pump and he could call the nurses to check in on Abigail. She had a seizure that first night and was put on anti-seizure medication and monitored closely.

My mom and dad developed a routine as well. They made the drive to the hospital at 5am so they could spend time with Abigail before we arrived for the day. They read books to their granddaughter, talked to her constantly, took photos for me, and told me she was so beautiful, every day. I knew she was beautiful, and I knew I loved her, but when three days went by and I still hadn't been able to hold my baby, I also knew I was missing out on those early bonding moments I had been so looking forward to. I had planned on being cuddled up with my new baby, doing skin-to-skin as much as possible and nursing her on demand. But not everything goes according to plan, as I was learning firsthand.

I remember my mom asking me one day at the hospital if I was feeling any pain, you know, from the birth. I must have just looked at her, expression blank and confused, because I couldn't answer, and then she understood. Any pain I was feeling in my body was masked by the deep emotional pain and emptiness I had in my heart and in my belly. I remember sitting in front of the TV at home with my husband in an attempt to keep my mind occupied elsewhere, and a commercial with a baby in it triggered me to break down in tears. I hugged and rubbed my once round and full tummy and sobbed, wishing Abigail was still inside me so that she could be safe again.

Abigail's MRI results were devastating. She suffered what the neurologists called Global Brain Insult, which meant that every part of her brain was affected. We wouldn't know for certain the extent of the injury until she grew older; however, the team believed it would be significant. I went numb. Our worst nightmare became our reality. The doctors were talking about palliative care for Abigail. She was in pain and this would be an option to keep her comfortable until she was ready to leave the world.

We rushed back to Abigail's room in the NICU and I demanded to hold my baby. The nurses sprang into action and made it happen. They put up a folding screen to give me privacy from the other families in the room, helped me put on a smock, and moved Abigail's wires and devices out of the way so I could hold her, skin to skin. With tears streaming down my face, I smiled at my baby and sung softly to her as I held her close. I never wanted to let her go. I believed I never would.

We were encouraged to go home that night and think about our choices. I couldn't comprehend what was happening — it still felt like a horrible nightmare. I remember asking my husband that night, "Why is this happening to us? What am I going to do? How will I spend my days? I have just closed a business so I can be one hundred percent present for our new baby, she would be my whole life, and now we have to give back our precious baby girl?"

The next morning, as I was once again hunched over Abigail's bedside, I noticed her foot twitch when I touched it — the first time I'd seen her move on her own. Later that day, when my sister was visiting, I saw Abigail's eyes open up a sliver, just long enough for me to catch a glimpse of their bright blue. I reported this to the nurses right away, and I'm not sure whether they believed me. But then she did it again, and this time my sister was my witness. Our little girl was waking up in a big way.

On day six, we arrived at the hospital bright and early as usual, and the nurses explained to us that they had done a spontaneous breathing test earlier that morning and Abigail started breathing, on her own! We were ecstatic. The following morning while the neurology team did their rounds, I was holding Abigail on my chest, and I remember looking over to see one of the head neurologists beaming at me. Something miraculous was happening.

My husband and I ensured we were at Abigail's bedside for every feed to prove to the doctors she would gain weight under our care. We were on a mission to get our baby home. We changed and weighed all her diapers, took her temperature, bathed her, and changed her outfits. We were operating as self-sufficient NICU parents.

One afternoon when the resident neurologist stopped by to visit, I asked him if we should be concerned that Abigail didn't cry. He gently flipped her on her tummy and noted that she did in fact get upset, that this was normal for someone who had been through as much as she had, and she should eventually start to develop a voice of her own.

On day thirteen, a plan was put in place to discharge Abigail from the NICU and send us home the next day. The doctors were so pleased with Abigail's clinical progress that they weaned her off all medication and repeated the MRI just to be sure their initial findings were correct. To our disappointment, the results of the MRI remained the same.

My husband and I made a promise to one another not to look online and try and diagnose our daughter. We decided early on that we would let Abigail dictate what she can and cannot do and that nothing Dr. Google says would change how we look at or treat our baby girl. She is her own person, and she is a fighter. Abigail was two weeks old when we left Sick Kids hospital and began the rest of our journey as parents to a beautiful little girl with huge blue eyes, strawberry blonde hair, and a will to live.

I hadn't taken the time to rest or recover since Abigail's birth and was up on my feet hours after she was born. I had dangerously high blood pressure until the day we took her home because of the stress, which landed me in emergency. I battled a fever and chills most nights after our hospital visits. But even though I was physically and emotionally exhausted, I had unwavering patience and strength for my baby girl.

When we arrived home from the hospital, I took Abigail upstairs into my bedroom, climbed into bed with her on my chest, and let her fall asleep on me. This was how it should have been.

The weeks that followed were especially challenging. Abigail slept in a bassinet beside our bed and because she didn't cry, I was up most nights watching her, waiting for her to wake for her feeds. I hired a lactation consultant to help me try and breastfeed Abigail, but she lacked the natural rooting reflex most babies are born with and had difficulty latching. I knew it wasn't working and after a week of stress, frustration, anxiety, and more tears, I decided to stop nursing and pumped exclusively. When Abigail was six weeks old, I was giving her a bath and as her skin touched the water, I heard a noise — one little mewled cry. The next day, she cried faintly a few times in a row. She was finding her voice! I remember being in the NICU rocking her in the glider and whispering to her that I didn't care if she cried all day or never slept, just as long as she was home with me.

Milestones would come and go, and as predicted, there were some undeniable delays. I ignored the milestone charts and deleted all the baby growth apps I had downloaded on my phone. Abigail would develop her fine and gross motor skills when she was ready, on her own terms. We began physiotherapy sessions once a week, sometimes twice, and were supported through the community with occupational therapy and an early childhood educator (ECE).

Abigail was diagnosed with cerebral palsy (CP) at her one-year follow up with the neurology team. We learned that there are varying degrees of CP and we wouldn't know where she stands for at least another year. The diagnosis changed nothing for us. We continued with weekly physiotherapy. Abigail started sitting independently, we enrolled her in a half-day preschool program at a school that supports children with special needs, and I found out I was pregnant with our second baby girl, Isla.

It had always been my dream to have two little girls — sisters who would be best friends, just like my sister and me. I was certain I had manifested this second baby girl, as I had daydreamed about bringing a lifelong guardian into the world for Abigail, someone who would be by her side, even after I leave this earth. The girls were born twenty-two months apart, just like my sister and me.

Today, Abigail's language and understanding are on par with that of a typically developing child her age; however, she's not able to form the words to express herself and thus relies on non-verbal gestures, some sign language, and a dedicated device to communicate with us. Although she is not yet speaking or walking independently, she is thriving and every day that passes, we are blown away with her progress and strong will to do more. I know without a doubt that she will walk and talk when she is ready and that she will accomplish anything she puts her mind to.

I still have flashbacks from my first birth experience almost every night, and I often struggle to not place blame on anyone. Despite the many un-answered questions about my journey, and the bits and pieces I will never understand, I always come back to these words: She is home.

Our days are full of toddler meltdowns and temper tantrums, smiles, laughter, and a lot of cuddles. I try my best to teach our girls how to share, be kind, and love one another. I am so grateful for my sweet Abigail Grace. She is an incredibly smart, strong, and caring little girl who lights up every-one around her and doesn't miss a thing. I can't wait to see what she does next! Abigail is proof that a mother's intuition will never lie and that a positive mindset has the power to create miracles.

So, Mama, trust your heart, know that miracles are possible, never stop fighting for, and believing in your children, and when you feel like it's all too much to bear, know that you've got this — you *always* have.

~ To my beautiful Abigail Grace. You will always be our little miracle. Thank you for teaching me patience and for showing me what unwavering love truly feels like. May you always dream big and love yourself unconditionally, for you are a special gift to this world. To my loving husband Chris, I couldn't have persisted through our journey without your hand in mine. You are my rock. And lastly to my own beau-tiful mom, your example of always leading with a positive attitude and full heart is the best gift you could ever give me.

8

NOTE TO SELF:
YOU MADE IT

by *Jessica Lance*

"Mamas can find beauty in the ugly, light in the darkness, and glitter in the poop."

Jessica Lance

Jessica Lance is a passionate, driven woman who jumps into everything in life with both feet. She thrives on a challenge and takes the leadership role in her own life. With much drive, Jessica graduated high school early at sixteen years of age to go on to community college. After her studies in diagnostic medical sonography, she took a couple years off and traveled the East Coast alone, living in several states including Florida and North Carolina. Upon returning to her home state of Illinois, Jessica met her husband, Tim. The two married and now have five children, including twins with cerebral palsy. Jessica spends her days assisting families to navigate the deep seas of special needs parenting, advocating for the rights of disabled individuals, and educating about the use of medicinal cannabis. When she's not trying to save the world, she dreams of owning a quiet homestead. She also enjoys painting, reading, and gardening. She runs a successful custom art and paint night business.

www.Icraveasimplelife.wordpress.com
ig: @eccentricbyjessica
fb: @werockcp | @eccentricbyjessica | @eccentricstorm

*"You aren't what's happened to you, you are how you've
overcome it."*
~Beau Taplin

ow could we be talking about the ending before our story began? It
felt as if we were given the last page of a novel, with the first twenty
chapters all blank. Everything we had imagined for our children felt out
of reach.

At just four short months postpartum from my first pregnancy, we found
out we were expecting again. I was nursing and hadn't had a menstrual cycle
yet. Birth control wasn't even on our radar, but neither was another pregnancy! Never in my wildest dreams did I imagine this could be possible. The first
call I made was to my obstetrician. After the birth of our eldest, the doctor
had recommended waiting for at least a year before we tried to conceive
again to lower the risk of complications to myself or another baby.

We waited the four weeks until we could go in for an ultrasound to make
sure it was a healthy, viable pregnancy. When the time came, the ultrasound
tech led us into a dark room and had me lie on the table. I remember thinking she was silent and not long after, she said she needed to consult with
our physician. I looked at my husband and in a moment of panic said, "We
must be miscarrying. It's too soon and they told us this could happen." Our
doctor came in and took over our sonogram. She said, "Well, guys, here is
baby number one and here is baby number two . . ."

Please quit counting is all I could get out before my husband and I burst into hysterics.

Here we were, only four months out from my first pregnancy with a four-month-old still in a pumpkin seat, sitting by my husband's feet, and a five-year-old (my stepson) at home, with two more babies on the way. Our doctor explained that the pregnancy was six weeks and one day old. I had tested positive just days after conception, which isn't uncommon with multiples. She explained that they were monochorionic diamniotic, identical twins, which meant they shared a placenta but not an amniotic sac and that we would need to be monitored closely. It also meant we would have a maternal-fetal specialist added to our team. Cue the waterworks and complete panic. My mind raced.

*We need a bigger house. We need a larger, more dependable vehicle. We need two more cribs, two more bouncy seats, two more swings, and will need to do twice as much laundry because we were having **two** more babies!*

At fourteen weeks gestation, our team monitored us for a potential complication that can arise with our type of twins. Sure enough, two weeks later, they confirmed we had it. Twin-to-twin transfusion syndrome. One of our twins was stealing the blood supply from the other, stealing amniotic fluid, and compromising our entire pregnancy. They took us to a little room and told us that Baby A was our recipient, also known as "the thief," and Baby B was the donor, "the victim." Baby A was swimming in an excess pool of fluid, causing an enlarged heart, excess cranial fluid, and a slew of other complications, while Baby B was in renal failure, with just enough fluid to urinate, swallow, and repeat. He was essentially plastic-wrapped in the amniotic sack, dehydrating himself before he even took his first breath. The doctor explained the science behind it saying, "It's just one of those things. A fluke. A one-in-a-million pregnancy with a one-in-a-million complication."

With our then-eight-month-old in tow, we asked so many questions we didn't want to ask. *What happens if we do nothing? Do we have options? What are our chances of survival? Does this compromise my health?*

My world was spinning. *How could this be happening? What did we do to deserve this? Why us? Why me? Why them? What did I do to make this happen? Did I not eat the right things? Did I not take something I should have? Was it the nausea medication or the nights I fell asleep before I took my prenatal supplements?*

These tiny, helpless babies hadn't even seen the light of day, felt the sun on their skin, smelled their mother's scent, felt my touch. We didn't even know if they were little boys or little girls. All we knew was that the two little babies inside my belly were dying inside me because my placenta didn't grow the way it should have to support two babies instead of one.

As we sat in a daze, our physician explained our options. We had a few. We could choose expectant management, which meant letting nature take its course. She said that no one would judge me or fault me for allowing this to happen. But that was a lie. I was judging me. I felt as though it were my fault this was happening. Isn't it crazy how we, as women and mothers, assume fault or feel inadequate? It was entirely chance. A random mutation. I had already carried to full term (forty-two weeks gestation to be exact!) and delivered one healthy, nine-pound baby boy. My body knew what it was doing. In my heart, I knew this was not my fault, but my head kept telling me otherwise. I couldn't shake the feeling it was MY fault and MY burden. I felt like my husband was judging my inadequacy. *His part of the job went swimmingly, and here my body as a woman couldn't even keep my babies alive inside me. How the hell was I going to take care of three infants if they even survived?*

My doctor continued on as my head spun with these thoughts. Option number two would be a series of amnioreduction, similar to amniocentesis, in which they would attempt to use a needle, guided by ultrasound, to remove some of the excess fluid from Baby A's side of placenta in the hopes of taking pressure off Baby B. Option number three was the most invasive. It included traveling six hours through different states to have intrauterine surgery to sever the blood supply between the two babies.

These babies had names. They had personalities already. Baby A was feisty and Baby B always nestled up in my ribs, giving me blows to the lungs, reminding me they were still alive and kicking. In my heart, I knew I couldn't let these babies die and felt an unexplainable need to prove to my husband, and to myself, that I was a good mother. I would do anything for my babies. They were mine, and I wasn't letting go.

We consulted with our obstetrician and tried the least invasive route first: amnioreduction. We did two rounds at sixteen weeks and eighteen weeks gestation, removing over six liters of fluid from my abdomen. The fluid caused so much pain and discomfort. Once it was removed, I would experience a few days of relief until it continued to come back again and again.

During this time, my team did genetic testing on the babies with the fluid recovered. We found out while they had a placental abnormality, they were genetically perfect. Identical baby boys. It was so real. We were no longer talking about fetuses in distress but rather about Gavin and Gabriel: my baby boys.

We were left with option number one, losing the babies we were fighting for, or option three — surgery.

My husband stayed behind with our now nine-month-old Ethan, who had just taken his first steps, who was still nursing even through all the chaos of the twins, who still co-slept with me every night tucked into the crook of my elbow. I felt as though I were being robbed of Ethan's infancy. I was missing moments and preoccupied with the twins' pregnancy care. I was there, but not in the way I wish I had been. Having so much discomfort and fluid in my abdomen stole bath time from me, laying on the floor watching him stack his first blocks, even being able to reach down and pick him up when he was upset and just wanted the comfort of his mother. We felt cheated and robbed by twin-to-twin transfusion syndrome.

My mom came with bags packed, ready to go. I had to be away from both my husband and my nursing baby for the first time to help our twin babies survive. It was an unbearable and uncomfortable six-hour drive. But armed with false bravado and the strength only a mother could have, I was on a mission to save my babies.

We arrived and met with our team of physicians, only to find out we had a ninety-percent chance of bringing one baby home, a sixty-percent chance of bringing two babies home, and a forty-percent chance I could lose one or even both of my babies. We also discussed what would happen if the babies came early. At just twenty weeks, they wouldn't survive.

We discussed what would happen if one of the twins died during surgery. This meant I would have to carry my child, who would be born asleep, inside me until his brother decided it was time to be born. At twenty weeks, my body would partially "reabsorb" him, meaning I may not deliver him or part of him at all. The thought of my body stealing my baby from me, disgusted me. My mind knew it was beyond my control, but my heart felt like my body had already betrayed me once, how dare it betray me again. We signed paperwork about transferring "medical waste," also known as my babies' bodies, across state lines if they were to pass and I delivered them in Ohio. I had to prepare for the thought of my living babies, nestled inside my stomach, losing their lives, one breath at a time.

Surgery came and went. I was awake during the procedure, lightly sedated but awake, with an epidural for pain management. I remember the medical jargon as I tried to relax, our lives in the medical team's hands. The anesthesiologist sat by my head and told me to carefully open my eyes and look up.

There he was. Gavin. Hairless and translucent. His eyelids looked fused shut and his nostrils were filled and not yet open. His little mouth was opening and closing. Then there was his hand. Those long, spindly fingers with his tiny, little wrinkly palms on the big television above my head.

This was my baby. The one I almost lost. It wasn't a black-and-white ultrasound picture. This was him. The one I felt flipping and kicking my bladder at 3am. The one stealing from his brother. The one who had his whole life ahead of him. I remember praying to God that if we made it, I would do whatever I could to make sure both he and his brother lived the best life they possibly could.

They told us that the first twenty-four hours post-surgery are pivotal. The next morning, the ultrasound technician came in and told us this was it. We would see two hearts beating, God willing, and there they were.

For ten more amazing weeks, I kept those babies inside me with the help of my family. We went home with orders of strict bedrest, monthly OB check-ups, and weekly appointments and ultrasounds with the maternal fetal specialist (MFM) to ensure the babies remained stable. I could only get up to shower once a day and to use the restroom. My days were filled with Netflix binges, library books, baby cuddles, and massive amounts of guilt with Ethan. The plan was to get us to thirty-five weeks before we delivered in order to give the boys their best chances at a complication-free birth.

On August 1st, 2012, I went in for my thirty-week check-up, complaining of pain. They did a stress test and said that it was normal to have abnormal contractions with twins and to just take it extra easy until my appointment with MFM the next day.

I couldn't sleep that night. By 5am, my pain worsened. My husband helped me stay comfortable until our 9am ultrasound with the MFM. Upon arrival, they found I suffered a full placental abruption with no cervical dilation — I had massive internal hemorrhaging. The babies weren't in distress, so they admitted me and administered steroids for the babies' lung development and a medication to stop the contractions. Thirty weeks was still early for these babies to arrive into the world; they needed another five weeks to have the best chance, but it didn't look like we would make it.

Not long after they administered the steroids, they told my husband to head home and grab our bags because we would deliver later that day. Shortly after he left, I felt odd. I paged the nurse in. Suddenly I couldn't hear anything; like the fuzzy sound of pure silence, it all faded away, and then my world went pitch black. My sister arrived as back-up just as I went into shock from the bleeding.

Machines beeping non-stop, codes being yelled, the rapid response team made their way to my room. My sister explains it like a movie. Everything happening in slow motion with people moving as fast as they can, like fighting through the crowd. They pushed her aside and asked her to wait outside as she watched through the glass window, her big sister helpless in the hands of the nurses and doctor.

When I regained consciousness, I was being straddled by a nurse on my stretcher as they pushed me to the operating room. She was trying to find the twins' pulses — and couldn't. The OR team or room, I'm not sure which, wasn't entirely prepared so they sat me up and administered an epidural. They left several voicemails for my husband, but he was not reachable.

I remember *that* moment vividly. The beeping of the machines, the copper smell of blood and flesh. I felt as if an elephant were sitting on my chest as they called out, "Here's Baby A, here's Baby B." They had made my incision very large and pulled the very tiny boys out together at the same time.

The room fell silent and time stood still. We made it. We're here. The day we've been waiting and working for and dreaming about.

Why was everything so quiet?

I remember calling out, "Why aren't they crying? Why aren't they cry-ing? Hello?" My questions were left hanging in the air, as the babies were now everyone's number one priority. I waited as they rushed them off to the Neonatal Intensive Care Unit (NICU) with no answer, no warm kiss on the forehead for a job well done, no comfort for the hell I had endured and what I had just lost, the pregnancy and birth experience that was stolen from me.

The medical staff reassured me, "They will be okay. They're in the best hands." *But how could they be in the best hands if they weren't with me?*

After they sewed me back together and took me to my room, I was reunited with my husband. He was told that the boys had ingested and as-pirated such a large volume of blood that it could have only been maternal. If it had been theirs, they would have bled out. They were without oxygen when I went into shock, had taken in all the blood, and were likely to have damage from it.

These boys, whom I fought so diligently to deliver whole and alive, came into this world broken. We were told days later that they suffered brain bleeds and had injuries called periventricular leukomalacia, which would like-ly cause cerebral palsy and seizure disorders. We spent thirty-five days in the NICU before we finally got to take them home.

Hindsight is always twenty-twenty. *What if they had delivered them right when I got there? What if the OB had done an ultrasound the day before their birth? What if I would've gone in at 5am instead of waiting for our 9am appointment?*

If I have learned anything from these boys, it's this: You can't live in the "what ifs." Asking "what if?" means living a scary place of asking for the un-obtainable. I had two living, breathing, beautiful baby boys, and another two at home. My life, even if it wasn't what I envisioned it to be, was filled with more love than I could ever imagine.

We were living life. The days came and went — some long, some passing by rather quickly. There were the usual sleepless nights. I had three children under the age of one and a five-year-old stepson; I was just trying to survive. My husband worked full-time, which meant I breastfed these three boys and zombie-shuffled through these days mostly alone. The boys were growing so fast. The twins learned and developed skills but then lost them just as quickly.

When they were nine months old, we heard the words we knew were coming all along: cerebral palsy.

When the twins were diagnosed, we were told they would likely be able to walk but may have motor planning delays. This means their brains will think, just like ours, but their bodies will have a hard time listening. They would also likely have spastic rigid muscles forever. These tiny, beautiful humans were going to have to face a life harder than anything I had ever had to go through: daily therapy, assistive technology, adaptive equipment, wheelchairs, walkers, standing frames, orthotics.

By five years old, they've had thirteen surgeries, twenty-three special procedures, almost three thousand hours of physical, occupational, speech, vision, and developmental therapies. But they've done it all with a smile.

As a special needs' mom, I always hear, "I just don't know how you do it. You're super mom!" But the truth is, I don't have a choice and frankly, neither do the boys. Giving up is not an option. It wasn't then, and it certainly isn't now. If I don't do everything I promised God I would do for these babies when we made it through our pregnancy, I will have failed. This isn't the path we would have chosen or envisioned, but it's the one we were given. Their lives are just as important now as they were during their pregnancy, and we are planning on making the best of them.

When a child (or in our case, children) is diagnosed with a special need, there is grieving and so much guilt. I'm here to tell you, that's okay! The grief comes and goes just as quickly as you celebrate new firsts. Having identical twins with special needs is very challenging. Gavin, our Baby A, is more severe than Gabe, his younger twin. Gabe can walk unassisted, while Gavin requires full assistance in everything he does. However, he is intelligent and has a hilariously smart mouth.

I struggle the most when I see Gabe do things that Gavin can't, as Gavin watches. When Gabe is rummaging through the fridge for a snack, Gavin is yelling, "Mom, I'm thirsty, please get me a drink!" He is unable to self-propel his chair or use his fine and gross motor skills to get a glass. Gabe is able to get himself dressed in clothes he picked out himself, while I have to dress

Gavin, hoping he likes what I've picked for him.

But these heartbreaks are quickly overshadowed by the most amazing moments you'd never expect to be world-changing. Gavin just learned to blow bubbles at five years old, and it was just as magical as when our eldest, Ethan, took his first steps at nine months old or when Gabe took his first steps at fifteen months old.

When you are a mother, you learn to find beauty in the ugly, light in the dark, and glitter in the poop. You will find the strength you never knew you had to not only survive but to thrive, especially when you have people depending on you for their very existence. It can be incredibly exhausting, but you learn to love like you never thought possible. Nothing compares to a mother's love, trust me. You live just for the little moments in the long nights, small laughs, when they're at the edge of sleep and reach out for you just wanting to know that you're there.

When you are faced with losing all of these precious moments before they've even begun, you gain a newfound appreciation for the moments of tears spilled, the moments spent locked in the bathroom because you need to pee alone, just once, or that handprint on your clean black leggings. Because you almost didn't have them. Every day is so precious and never guaranteed. Kiss your babies, Mamas. They may be disguised as tiny dictators, but they're actually tiny miracles.

~ To my husband, Tim, who puts up with the crazy with a smile and unconditional love. To my kiddos, who have taught me that nothing is what you expect it to be but is beautiful in its own light.

9

ANXIETY:
THE INVISIBLE BARRIER

by Tia Slightham

"No one is "perfect";
don't let anyone
make you feel like
you're failing."

Tia Slightham

Tia is a teacher, business owner, and most importantly, a mom to her two adorable boys, Hudson, age nine and Beckett, age seven. She lives in Toronto, Canada where she balances her life being a wife, mother, and mompreneur. She has a master's degree in early childhood education (ECE) and taught kindergarten in the United States before moving to Canada.

Tia has found her passion working with kids and families for over fifteen years. Tia is the founder of *Tia Slightham - Parenting Solutions*, where she works with parents to teach them positive ways to decrease the daily struggles we all encounter as parents. Tia will work alongside you to tailor a plan best suited to your family's specific needs. The positive solutions will be effective and long-lasting and will help you and your child reconnect. Let's start talking!

www.tiaslightham.com
t: @tiaslightham
fb: @tiaslightham | ig: @tia_slightham

"When I let go of what I am, I become what I might be."
~ Lao Tzu

What makes us who we are as individuals and human beings? Is it genetics and characteristics passed down from generation to generation? Or are we simply a pure blank slate at birth, with each moment, event, and memory molding our being? Through my experience of being a teacher, parent, and parent consultant, I believe it's a combination of the two. What this means is some parts of who we are as individuals are set in stone. They are carved ahead of time. The rest is left to our environment: the family and household we grow up in and the experiences we go through — good and bad. The positive and negative repercussions of each event help create who we are.

Due to this combination of nature and nurture, I feel that part of my son's anxiety was already in his cards. Hudson's genetics dealt him the anxiety card, and he needed to play to win. I can't help but wonder if it was something I did to lead him toward this debilitating curse. I will never be sure of this, but the "what ifs" will forever roam my mind as I search for the answer. An answer I will most likely never find.

Watching your child suffer in any way is the most helpless feeling in the world. You feel in control one minute and out of control the next. Left with overwhelming feelings of hopelessness. Begging for anyone to help you get out of this moment in time when your child is suffering. What you wouldn't give in that instant to trade places with your child. In these moments, you feel alone and desperate for these feelings to stop. As your child suffers, you suffer, but you are the parent, the stronghold for your child and family. You are their rock, their support, their anchor and person to lean on. But through this suffering, you yourself can crumble; your strong edges slowly chip away, and you are left feeling completely lost.

Through earning my master's degree in early childhood education, teaching kindergarten, building my parenting business, and being a mama, I've gained lots of experience working with kids. Now you may be thinking to yourself, *It sounds like you're telling us you have it all figured out.* Well, I don't. Every parent, every child, and every household will have something. No one is "perfect," so don't let anyone make you feel like you're the only one failing while they pretend to have it all figured out. It's just not possible! There are too many cards in this deck of life and motherhood, and too many ways in which the cards we are dealt can create unwanted struggles and issues. We are all dealt the hand we are meant to play, but what matters most is *how* we play these cards.

I'd like to tell you about the cards our family was dealt: what it feels like to be caught in the middle of my son's anxiety tornado. What it feels like to be spinning with no end in sight, losing all sense of control.

Here's where our story begins. I am a type A personality and I like everything in order. We have charts and schedules in our home to keep everyone organized. We have consequences laid out in advance to keep the boys accountable for their daily duties and behavior choices. Everything is relatively predictable in the highest account.

When my first son, Hudson, was born, I spent hours ensuring I taught him to sleep well, created a healthy schedule, stimulated him with social classes, and helped him become a well-rounded and well-adjusted little boy. For my first round at being a mom, things seemed to be going well, but when Hudson was eighteen months old, I noticed he was becoming quite clingy. My husband worked extremely long hours, which meant that Hudson and I spent most of our time together. I figured this behavior was typical for the age. After all, every parenting book I dove into spoke of this: *separation anxiety.* I took what I thought was the right next step and signed him up for nursery school, believing this would be an opportunity for him to learn to be away from mommy, make new friends, and play. I thought this would be a happy time for Hudson, but he proved me wrong. I knew there would be a few tears when I left him in this new environment, but I wasn't aware of how bad it would actually be.

On his first day of school, Hudson cried and squeezed me with all his might, and I thought it would be short-lived. But every Tuesday and Thursday morning, for an entire school year, we had the same episode cycling over and over. My initial sense was that these outbursts would diminish over time, that he would get used to school and adjust. But none of this happened. Hudson's battle with anxiety was starting its spin cycle at this moment, but I was unaware. I thought this was developmentally appropriate and normal, having no idea how wrong I was. Unknowingly, I was deep at the bottom of a dark cave. Lost. Oblivious to what my little boy needed.

As Hudson grew, so did his anxiety. The hardest part for me was that I didn't know about it or recognize the signs. I was lost and willing to try anything to help Hudson feel more comfortable with typical things. When we went to parenting groups or classes, he wouldn't leave my side, but I kept trying. When we went for play dates, he needed me to stay with him, yet I insisted we keep going. He wouldn't attend birthday parties alone, so I went with him to support him. Hudson was so fearful to try to new things. Whenever I'd ask him if he would like to take a new fun class or attend a day camp, he would respond, "No!" No pauses or room for consideration. He was angry at the very thought of doing anything new and completely shut out these opportunities. My frustration was rising, and I couldn't understand why he was being so difficult. I didn't know at the time that these behaviours were symptoms of a much bigger problem.

Hudson is a bright, kind, and sensitive old soul. From the moment he was born, he was a little man. Very serious and extremely focused, inquisitive beyond his years. He is the sweetest, most tender being I know. My heart melts for him, and my desire for him to be understood burns bright. Externally, everyone sees Hudson as this perfect child. Behaviorally, he is compliant and always aims to please. What everyone doesn't see, however, is the anxiety that storms his body. This invisible disability that rules his world and overpowers his ability to relax and enjoy life. This internal secret that causes him to miss out. This anxiety was something I didn't know existed until he was seven years old. I can't believe that for seven whole years, he had this invisible barrier and I didn't know.

How could I have missed it? How did I not know what was going on? I am his mother; I should know him better than anyone else.

I felt like I failed Hudson. He needed me, and I wasn't there. He was counting on me to take care of him, to guide and help him when things weren't easy, yet I was blind to his actual needs. I had no idea that what he was suffering from during these moments was anxiety.

Being the type A personality mom, paired with the education I had, I developed some coping skills to help Hudson move beyond his fears. I continued to sign him up for sports and activities even though he resisted. Knowing that once he got there, he would feel proud of himself. The transition from point A to point B has always been the hardest part for Hudson. He has always needed a firm but gentle push to get him across the threshold. If he fought the anxiety and made it across, he would leave feeling successful. If he couldn't reach point B and his anxiety held him back, he would leave feeling like a failure.

As time went on, I continued to push, and he continued to resist. This became our way of life. I learned to expect the worst episode and be pleasantly surprised if the anxiety attack was minimal and not explosive. I asked myself *why* every time. *Why did this sweet little boy have to feel this way? What did I do wrong? Did I cause Hudson's anxiety and fears? Was it just in his cards? How can I make this stop?*

The hardest thing about your child having anxiety is the direct impact it has on you as a parent. Each time Hudson's anxiety struck, it caused anxiety in me, too. I could feel his pain and worry deep in my core. I worried that he would worry and that we would be stuck dealing with another outbreak. Continually walking on eggshells, wondering when the next heavy breathing, complete body and mind shut down, panic-stricken, out-of-body experience would occur. I felt scared and was unsure of how to proceed next. I had tried all my parenting tactics and exhausted all the tools in my parenting toolbox. I was failing Hudson, and the older he got, the more I realized there was nothing I could do. There was no quick fix. This was who he was. He would not outgrow it on his own, and I needed to face the facts. *My son has anxiety. This is not normal behavior and oh my God, he needs me.*

As time has passed, I grew to know that it wasn't me or anything I did that caused Hudson to have these dreaded anxiety attacks. This was part of Hudson, his deck of cards, and it helped make him, him. But that didn't mean anxiety had to define him or run his life. Watching him suffer and feeling his pain was more than I could take. Determined to help him learn to control and fight his anxiety head on, we worked together to beat these tornados that voraciously spun inside his little body.

The pivotal moment, which helped me realize that these episodes were not "normal" and were not something I caused, came on a cool January morning. It was the morning of Hudson's grade three private school placement exam. It wasn't the exam that stressed Hudson. What stressed Hudson was the drop-off at a new place without me. It was his fear of not knowing in advance how the morning would look. He needed to know every detail about every situation, but even with this information, he would often spiral into his anxiety attacks. Once again, transitioning from point A to point B was going to be difficult.

On this particular morning, he was demonstrating his typical anxiety signs. I suspected they would be present, but I hoped with my entire being that this day would be different, that they wouldn't show up. As he sat to eat his breakfast, the symptoms began.

"Mommy, my tummy hurts. Mommy, I don't want to go. Mommy, why do I have to go?"

This is how Hudson's tornados began. As I answered his questions, all with answers he didn't want to hear, his tornado spiraled faster and harder. The anxiety was taking over. Soon he stopped listening to what I was saying. He refused to go altogether. In a matter of minutes, he went from eating breakfast calmly to fighting his battle. Once again, stuck in the center of this emotional beast, with hot, sweaty tears pouring. No matter what I said or did, the tornado whirled within him. Once again, I was left feeling lost and helpless.

What am I supposed to do? How can I make this stop? Why Hudson and why me?

As I dropped him off, my insides felt like they were being pulled in opposite directions. My heart broke into a thousand pieces for Hudson. I wanted so badly to make this go away. I worried that in this moment, he would be judged for his external behaviours, without anyone knowing he was fighting an internal, debilitating disability. I feared he wouldn't be given a fair chance and might be viewed as a child who wasn't capable of managing his emotions. Knowing that he could be judged was enough to make me want to march back inside, take him into my arms, and make it all go away. But as we fought our way through this treacherous storm of anxiety, I knew that my arms around him wouldn't make it go away. Sure, I could go in and "save" him for the moment, but he wouldn't feel successful or good about himself after. I knew this time was no different than all the others. Hudson needed to get from point A to point B, which meant I needed to leave it up to him to make this transition on his own accord.

When I arrived to pick up Hudson, he was all smiles. He waved at me through the glass, and it took every fiber of my being to hold back my tears. I wanted to burst into an ugly cry and crumble to the ground. Hudson came running out to hug me and I squeezed him until he begged me to stop. He had made his transition and had a successful experience. In the end, he was offered a spot in the school and everything worked out.

The real reason this morning worked out wasn't because we were accepted into the school. Rather, it was because it acted as our moment of truth. I finally realized and accepted that Hudson didn't have normal worries and his little body was trying hard to cope with something much more. Something much more than either he or I had the capability to deal with alone. We needed help. This help would be the beginning of the end we had hoped to one day achieve. Since that cold January day, Hudson has worked with a child psychologist and a social worker at school. He adores his time with these professionals and for once, he feels understood; he feels normal and no longer feels alone. The best part is that he has people who know exactly how to support him.

My eyes swell with tears as I write my story, as I admit to feeling like I failed my son. For seven long years, I didn't know that my son had anxiety and for this, I will always have regrets. I will always and forever wish I had hindsight to decrease his pain and struggle. As Hudson and I have walked this journey together, we have learned to lean on each other. We have learned to listen to one another and forgive one another. We have talked about how sorry I am for not recognizing it sooner. Our bond is thicker than glue and stronger than nails.

Sometimes it's the tough times and the rocky patches in our parenting journey that bring us the most joy. It's these moments when we learn to genuinely appreciate what we have. Being a parent is the biggest, most beautiful, and best gift I have ever been given. It's not always the easiest gift to bear, but I know as I continue to unwrap layer upon layer of my kids, I become more complete. I have learned not to be so hard on myself. I am doing my best, and my best is enough. I have learned not to blame Hudson's behaviour or actions on myself. These are the cards he has been dealt, and I have been there to help him dig deep to find the roots of why this happens. To find the reasons why he has had this invisible barrier.

As I watch Hudson excel in school, swim competitively, and learn to discover what makes him truly happy, I know we will be okay. We continually work hard on his anxiety by practicing the tools we've learned. Sometimes we have setbacks, but we have more knowledge about how to deal with these moments.

Anxiety is a vicious cycle that repeats itself over and over again. It's not something that simply goes away. It needs YOU to take charge. YOU need to stand up, look it dead in the eye, and fight. Hudson has fought hard and learned to control his internal tornados. Today he pushes through, copes, and faces anxiety head on! I am so proud of his hard work, bravery, and strength. Anxiety won't stop Hudson from being all he can be. Together, we are chipping away at his invisible barrier, and hopefully one day it will disappear altogether. Through his journey with anxiety, we have learned to accept it, thrive with it, and appreciate it — without it, Hudson wouldn't be Hudson at all, and I wouldn't be the mama I am to him today.

~ This chapter, although it's short, represents so much more. It's a huge part of my life, my journey of motherhood. Thanks to my husband for his support, kindness, and eternal gentle love for our family.

To Hudson's little brother, Beckett, for always support-ing without an ounce of judgement when anxiety took over.

To Dr. Walker, for her wisdom and guidance.
'The biggest thanks of all to Hudson, for being one of the best things that's ever happened to me. You made me a mama, and you are the sweetest soul I'll ever know.

10

CANCER IS NOT A CHOICE, HAPPINESS IS

by Lisa Mechor

"Handling something boils down to your mindset and attitude, which is eighty percent of the battle."

Lisa Mechor

Lisa Mechor was born and raised in Saskatoon, Saskatchewan, Canada. She knew from a young age that she loved children and followed this path by pursuing a bachelor's degree in education. Although Lisa has lived in many cities within Canada, she shares a fondness for Vancouver, BC as some of her best memories with her family were created there, and it feels like another home away from home, and that is where her heart and soul is. She currently resides in Calgary, AB, which she lovingly calls home with her husband, Brad, and their seven-year-old son, Cole.

With a spirit and passion for the outdoors and the beauty of the Canadian prairies in her backyard, you will find Lisa on the tennis court, golf course, or ski hill! She also enjoys dining at favorite restaurants, indulging in a glass of champagne, and connecting with friends and family.

ig: @lmechor

"The strongest people I've met have not been given an easier life. They've learned to create strength and happiness from dark places."

~ Kristen Butler

In 2002, my dad was diagnosed with stage four brain cancer. There was no warning. He went from being at work one day to "You have a glioblastoma" the next. I took care of him for almost a year. There were many lessons in that year, both good and bad. I spent my time mainly with my dad and my family. I focused on enjoying each day with my dad and ensuring his days with us were as comfortable as possible. I shut out the rest of the world and didn't even tell anyone he was sick. I carried on with my day-to-day as though everything were normal. I had moved to Edmonton with my husband three months before my dad was diagnosed, but my parents had just separated so I moved back to Saskatoon. Whenever I saw familiar faces on the streets, at the grocery store, anywhere I went, my response was curt, saccharine sweet, and polite "Oh hi! Yes, we are just visiting town and we are doing fine, thanks." Only our closest friends and family knew my dad was sick. *I don't know why I did this; perhaps because it hurt too much to face the reality and gravity of what was happening.*

When my dad passed, I had a hard time carrying on my normal life when I returned to Edmonton; it was a whole year before I felt okay again. I wondered, *Will I ever feel happy again?*

Fast forward to 2007. We moved to Calgary from Vancouver (yes, we moved a lot) and we wanted to start a family. Let's just say this was not easy for me! I did three years of very challenging fertility treatments. I was one of their most expensive patients. They pumped me full of drugs and synthetic hormones, and my body would barely respond. So many failed attempts, heartbreak, days of endless frustration.

The day came when the doctors said that this would be my last IVF treatment, as it was too hard on my body. There was then a mix-up with the drugs, which was super frustrating because this was my last chance. My husband and I ended up on estrogen instead of antibiotics. He felt horrible, and I ended up getting infected from the IV line at my egg retrieval. Then I needed higher doses of antibiotics. To say that my hope and faith were shot down would be an understatement. I doubted we would ever get pregnant with this latest mishap.

Yet life had other plans for us. On May 28, 2010, we found out we were pregnant with our firstborn. After three years of trying, at age thirty-five, I finally saw that line on the pregnancy test confirming I was PREGNANT. We could not believe it!

I went for blood work to confirm and my doctors thought that with my hormone levels, it may be twins. An ultrasound confirmed that yes, indeed, we were having twins. At the later fourteen-week ultrasound, however, there was only one heartbeat. Although we were disappointed, we felt grateful to have that one healthy heartbeat.

My pregnancy did not go the way I envisioned; it was so challenging that a whole chapter wouldn't be enough to explain it. In fact, we were told to terminate the pregnancy after an amniocentesis at twenty-two weeks gestation. We made the decision that this was our baby and we would do everything we could to bring this life into the world.

I kept my entire pregnancy a secret. Hiding my belly under loose, baggy clothing and a barrelful of lies wasn't hard, since my physique was naturally petite. There were no celebrations, no baby shower(s), no shopping or nesting. Everything was one big secret to be kept under wraps until I delivered this baby.

I worried before each ultrasound, preparing for the worst-case scenario, but our little boy looked perfect! I went into labour three days before my due date. Additional doctors were on-call just in case they had to intervene. After twenty-seven hours of labour, on January 29, 2011, our healthy baby boy, Cole, was born! It was the best day of my life, and I could not believe how perfect he was. I asked Brad if he looked okay and he said Cole was beautiful. The doctors dismissed the team and we were transferred to our room. After an overnight stay at the hospital, we were released the next day and could finally take our new little bundle home! I could not believe it — he was ours and he was coming home with us. Away we went; I was finally a mom, we were finally parents! My excitement knew no bounds, and my love for our newborn was a feeling like no other.

Our little family of three was perfect. Every day, however, I wished my dad was here to watch his grandson grow up. Both my mom and sister were thrilled that we finally had our family. I kept thinking, *We are good, please let this be the end of all hardship!*

For some reason, we never get much warning with bad news — it always comes to us via a phone call, and BAM, there it is, something shocking and life-altering.

In August 2016, my mom went for a routine mammogram and they found "something." Soon after, she travelled to Europe; upon her return home, she had a confirmed diagnosis of invasive breast cancer. She would consult a surgeon to discuss her options.

What did this mean? Had it spread?

I already lost my dad — no way in hell this was happening to my mom. I flew back to Regina from Calgary and met my sister. Nobody was coping well with this news, but I resolved not to worry about anything until we knew all the details. I was determined to be my family's cheerleader and ensure we were busy with fun distractions.

At her appointment, she was told the cancer was in the early stages. She could have a double mastectomy and reconstruction and then no further treatment would be needed as it had only spread within the breast tissue. She would need a thirteen-hour surgery but would be cancer free post-surgery and recovery. She had the surgery, and although there were complications, after about nine months, she was traveling again and living life. We were so grateful. I still have my happy and healthy mom. We are very close, chatting at least a few times a day. That experience made me a firm believer in early detection.

Since we had so many cancer diagnoses in our family, it was suggested that I go to a genetic counselor and get tested for the cancer gene. I took Cole to that meeting, as I had no childcare options that day. He sat there as I debriefed the doctor on my family history with cancer. I let him know that my dad, my uncle, my mom, my grandmother, and my grandfather all had cancer and they all (with the exception of my mother) had passed away. A naturally curious young boy, Cole asked lots of questions at the appointment; hindsight is always twenty-twenty. I wish I hadn't taken him to the appointment. Of course he was worried! He didn't know what cancer was, but he didn't want me to have it, and neither did I. My worst fear has always been leaving my son and my husband; the thought of not being there to see my little boy grow up and my husband and I grow old together breaks my heart.

Three weeks after the test, it was confirmed I did not have any genes that would increase my risk of a cancer diagnosis. Thank goodness! They asked if I would like to get Cole tested. Since I was okay, I figured he would likely fare the same. I thought, *Why would I have my six-year-old tested? No, he will be fine, he is so healthy!*

Then we came to the summer 2017. Cole wasn't feeling great; he had recurring ear infections and fevers that did quite a number on him, as well as us. When he started school in September, he had trouble with stamina and maintaining his energy levels through the day. He could not walk up the steps of the school with a backpack; it seemed too heavy and he felt weak, constantly complaining of pain in his legs and arms. Cole also wasn't gaining weight; in fact, he seemed to be losing more weight as the weeks went by.

Should grade one be so tiring?

His colour was not good, his skin tone now pale, ashen, and bruised. I set up an appointment with our pediatrician to chat about how he was finding school and how he was feeling. She said, "He does look pale, but it might just be that time of year when we are all pale." She gave me a requisition form to get a complete blood count (CBC) completed. Cole was tired that day, so we had a nice lunch out and then he went home to relax. He went to school the following morning.

I was worried about him, thinking about everything we went through to have him, the pregnancy, the labor, all the scares. I will always worry about him and hold him close. When I went to pick him up after school, I found him in tears, telling me he felt weak and tired. I took his backpack and put him in the car. We went to the Alberta Children's Hospital and headed straight to the lab to get our blood work done. He did great, no tears whatsoever. After the appointment, I asked if he would like a treat from downstairs for being so brave. He said, "No, Mommy, I am fine, let's go home."

It was a cold day and we were exhausted from our trip to the hospital. We were having dinner and relaxing by the fire when my cell phone rang. *Here we go again*, I thought. The phone call was from an on-call doctor with our pediatric group.

She said, "You were at the lab today, the results came back. Your son has blood cancer, you need to pack your bags and go directly into emergency once you arrive at the hospital, where you will be admitted. You need to get there within thirty minutes and will be staying for a few nights at least. There will be an oncologist on site to meet you."

WHAT?

In sheer shock and disbelief at what this might mean, I said, "I am sorry, can you please repeat all this information to my husband? He is a doctor and I am not sure I heard you correctly." Brad took over the phone call and had the news conveyed to him as well. I looked at Cole curled up by the fire, all warm, cozy, and restful. My heart broke as I said, "Sweetie, we have to go to the hospital again for a little bit, as they want to make sure you are okay." I packed him a bag, grabbing nothing for myself, and feeling completely numb, like a robot, went through the motions of getting us ready and off to the ER.

I didn't cry. I could not process this.

Lisa, you've got this keep going. This is not the first bad news we have had. Do what they tell us and take it one step at a time. Lisa, you've got this.

We arrived at the ER only to find out Cole's blood counts were so off the charts, they could not believe he was alert and looking as good as he did.

They started an IV line immediately; we noticed how swollen his neck was and huge his lymph nodes were! It looked like he had no neck. His fever was high, and he was so sick. *How did I, his mother, not notice this all?* They said they would confirm what type of cancer he had in the morning and admitted us to oncology. Cole underwent every test under the sun that night; it felt like we didn't sleep because it was just test after test.

The next morning, his diagnosis was confirmed. Cole had high risk acute lymphoblastic leukemia. It was categorized as high risk because his white blood cell count was so high. I couldn't believe my baby was so sick. He was scheduled for surgery in two days. They would do a port (implant), a bone marrow biopsy, and a lumbar puncture. We waited all day on Friday until we were finally called to the operating room (OR) at 3pm. I got to take him in and hold him as he went under. We were all so scared; there were many tears, but in my heart, I just kept hoping and praying he would be okay. I kissed him and walked out of the OR. I had not left the hospital for two days and his surgery would last about two hours, so we stepped out for some air. We went to grab a bite to eat and as we were walking back in to the hospital, my cell phone rang.

"Is this Cole's mom?"

I replied, "Yes," barely able to breathe.

"I am calling to let you know there has been a complication in the OR with Cole's airway. He had a difficult airway due to swelling in his neck (lymph nodes); as a result, we had to intubate him."

What? Another phone call with bad news? Why does this keep happening?

The doctor said that Cole was stable and would be moved to the intensive care unit (ICU). *How could this have gone from bad to worse?* We got to Cole's room in the ICU; *that* was not something I was prepared for. Seeing your child hooked up to a breathing machine, hands restrained so he could not take the tube out.

Now I had seen the worst. How could this be happening? Why us? Why Cole?

They were making all sorts of decisions and said they felt starting chemo that evening would be best. *How could they administer chemotherapy to a sedated child on a breathing machine?* I wondered. Well, they did. In walked the gowned nurses who looked like they were wearing hazmat suits and administered Cole's first dose of chemo. It was unreal to me how the week had gone.

The hospital staff took excellent care of Cole in the ICU and decided that Sunday morning would be the time to try and take the breathing tube out. They had to wean him off the drugs so he could breathe on his own. Cole, on the other hand, wanted to pull the tube out on his own. At around 10am, the doctors took out the tube. Cole coughed and struggled initially, but he was breathing on his own. He asked for his teacher (Mrs. K) and then his iPad! He was okay, thank goodness.

We ended up staying in the hospital after a few other complications for almost six weeks. This is when I had to put all of the coping skills I had been working on to the test. For the first time, I *had* to allow people to help out. I *had* to tell them what was going on and *allow* them to help. I have the most amazing friends and family who stepped up. In order for me to help Cole, I had to be vulnerable and let my walls down. It was really hard in the beginning, but once I allowed people to help, there were lunches delivered, quick visits to cheer us up, rides to the mall to pick up the things we needed, text messages, phone calls, and people spoiling us. Every single one of these gestures helped us cope with our new life. Without allowing friends and family in, I do not know what we would have done.

We knew that life outside the hospital could and would be very isolating. Due to the severe and constant doses of chemotherapy, Cole is neutropenic, which means he can't fight infection. As such, we came up with new things to do in our new lifestyle.

I figured that all we needed were things to look forward to. We could not see anyone or go anywhere, so we had to find new ways of having fun. We did it! It became a challenge that kept me busy. I focused on things that would distract us, and Brad was on board with whatever we came up with. I decided that since we could not go to restaurants, I would convert the back of my SUV into a place for picnics. I even bought us all matching boots for our tailgate picnics. We loved it! We would find a spot with a view, pop the hatch, and enjoy our lunch with blankets in the fresh air.

We started saying yes to meal drop-offs and to people offering to do things for us or come by for a quick visit. I tried not to focus on the challenging parts of the day and instead, chose to focus solely on the positive aspects.

I have always asked Cole at the end of each night what the best part of his day was. He still had lots of love for life and was having fun each day. I think that's a gift and a good lesson. Cole was *not* focused on having cancer — he was focused on the *fun* that we were having. It's amazing to me.

Even now, he doesn't worry, so I try to not worry either and take it one day at a time. I have to say, it's working. Our lives are simple. We wake up, have time with each other, try to have some fun, and then do it all over again the next day. We don't think about what we are not doing right now; we think of the new things we have been doing. How you handle something really boils down to your mindset and attitude about it, which is eighty percent of the battle. No matter what is going on, it could be worse. We are grateful and always will be. Although why we had to learn some of these lessons, I will never know.

Cole is growing up to be such a strong, resilient boy, and I hope he continues to be able to cope with anything life throws at him. It took me many years to learn this, but I am glad that I had lessons along the way to prepare me for this. I am strong. I am enough. It is okay for me to reach out to my village for help. I do not give up, and I want to embody and exemplify this for Cole. I have tons of energy to pour into things and can focus on the positive. We are handling this cancer diagnosis, and we are doing it very well! We also choose to surround ourselves with others that can do this, too. It's sad when people cannot find joy in simple things and really focus on what matters. We do not love cancer, but we LOVE our lives and each other.

~ I dedicate this chapter to my son Cole, who has taught me so much in seven years about life and how to live life to its fullest! To my very supportive loving husband, Brad, to my mom and sister, who are always there for me, and to my amazing girlfriends for carrying me through one of the hardest years of my life. I love you all.

Section 3
EMBRACING THE IMPERFECT JOURNEY

FEATURING

Meghan Krmpotic

Nia Pycior

Justine Dowd

Taelar Howe

Danielle Williams

OPENING COMMENTARY BY

Sabrina Greer

My experiences with fertility, pregnancy, miscarriage, and loss are not the same as the brave warriors whose stories you are about to read.

I was one of the *lucky ones* who got pregnant fairly easily and had wonderful, dreamy, risk-free pregnancies. Sure, there was puking, cramping, and fear of the unknown; my abs split, my ass grew four sizes, and after fifty-six hours of grueling labour, I had to get stitches on my lady parts, but I honestly can't complain and wouldn't change a thing. My children are here, they are healthy, and they are perfectly imperfect. I say this not to brag or rock the boat of someone already riding through turbulent waters; no, I say this to announce that I am not qualified to speak to the topics of infertility, loss, and grief. This is one more reason why I chose to share this space with twenty-one other mamas. I do not have all the answers. I have not gone through all the things. We all have a story, we all have a journey, and we can all learn from the challenges, struggles, and experiences of others.

In reading the next five chapters, I learned a myriad of valuable lessons. First, to be more empathetic. You never truly know what others are going through, and asking questions such as, "When is baby number two coming?" or "Why don't you have kids yet?" is not very sensitive to those potentially fighting a silent battle.

I also learned to squeeze my little ones tighter and love them a little harder because, regardless of how crazy they drive me, they are a blessing, and some other woman might be going through hell in an attempt to have exactly what I have. On the days when my three healthy sons are screaming, arguing, and trashing the house, I remind myself that these are the very moments another woman might be longing for. Perspective is a gift and one you will surely be given in the next five chapters.

I've learned that the only time we can truly conquer our darkness is when we allow light in. To do that, we need to open up, share our truths unapologetically and unashamed, and stand for each other in solidarity. Dr. Brené Brown (who specializes in vulnerability studies) says, *"Vulnerability is not winning or losing. It's having the courage to be seen when we have no control over the outcome."* Being vulnerable is uncomfortable. It can make us feel exposed and terrified. However, when we share our truths and our stories vulnerably, like the courageous women in this book, we can be the light for others. You will see this theme throughout this book. One of our authors, Nia Pycior, says it so eloquently:

"Maybe it's not that misery loves company, per se; it's that we just need to see our pain reflected in someone else's story. A collective consciousness, an inspired, empowered, yet raw and honest sharing of our experiences as women, wives, mothers. There is no power in silent suffering or silent rejoicing. There is power in vulnerability; be the misery that company loves."

So while my experience differs from the next, I see you, Mama.

To the women desperate for a child, all-consumed with appointments, injections, and continuous disappointments — We see you. To the mamas seeking rainbows after a horrific storm, remember that you cannot have rainbows without rain. To the mamas suffocating in grief, who have had to do the unimaginable and say goodbye to a little one far too soon, you are a warrior, you are not alone, and we see you, too. And to all the mamas who continue to brave societal judgment and insensitivity on your fertility journey — please know that you are enough. You are not any less of a woman, a mother, a warrior goddess. You are everything and more. We see you, Mama, and we've got your back.

11

THERE IS GLORY
IN THE GORY

by Nia Pycior

"It's not that misery loves company; we just need to see our pain reflected in others."

Nia S. Pycior

Nia is the product of a Jamaican mother and an American father and takes great pride in her Caribbean roots. Her heritage is often reflected in her diverse perspective on many topics, as well as in outbursts of Patois (Jamaican dialect) when excited, startled, or upset. Nia is always analyzing her life from the perspective of her deathbed, a habit that stemmed from her six years as a hospice social worker. This is how she determines if something is worth doing, saying, or risking. With that in mind, she started a blog, *Perfect for the Pocket,* where she shares her thoughts on various subjects, including her journey through infertility and in-vitro fertilization (IVF) in order to banish the stigma, shame, and loneliness that can shroud this health condition. She's been a stay-at-home mama for over a year, and she spends her days managing her vivacious and dramatic one-year-old daughter and expecting her second baby, a son, in a few months! In between household duties and daydreaming about the next meal, she fights her natural introverted tendencies by deliberately maintaining a social life. Nia has been married to the love of her life for seven years and lives within minutes of all her in-laws, whom she adores. She is passionate about her faith, family, and good food and enjoys a glass of single malt Scotch, neat. She considers herself a constant work in progress and hopes to be remembered for trying to help others by being vulnerable and sharing her experiences.

www.perfectforthepocket.com
ig: @niasherika
fb: Nia (Manning) Pycior

*"Vulnerability is our most accurate
measurement of courage."*

~ Brené Brown

hat does one say when given a platform to share their message? If I never get the chance to say anything ever again, what would my last words be? Being the daydreamer I am, I have thought about this question for years. Ideally, the platform would be Oprah's talk show (back in the day) or *The Ellen DeGeneres Show*. I'd fan girl for a minute, and then I would tell her there is something I needed to say to the world. I would look directly into the camera and tell everyone listening that they matter, their lives matter, their stories matter, they are worthy of love, and they are enough. Instead, my platform is emails to my girlfriends, text messages, and my blog — a far cry from a popular talk show — and my audience is other women on their way to motherhood and women who are already mothers.

My particular story isn't remarkable or extraordinary, but it's no less worthy of sharing. Once you have experienced infertility, you know the grasp of its cold clutch. Some women may feel like they've been grabbed by a toe, while others have felt its grasp upon their hearts, their minds, every fiber of their being. I am not the first, nor will I be the last, woman to experience infertility. It is a world awash in appointments, pills and injections, diminishing bank accounts, newly acquired loans, fancy medical jargon, vaginal ultrasounds, phone calls, and procedures of varying levels of invasiveness — the poking, the prodding, the mental, emotional, and physical anguish that you go through all because you know you are meant to be a mother. These things are familiar to women who have used medical interventions to help them conceive. It's all very clinical, Google-able stuff.

After a diagnosis of Polycystic Ovarian Syndrome (PCOS) and two failed intrauterine inseminations (IUI), in-vitro fertilization (IVF) became the method by which we had our first child and hope to have a second in about four months. In the mix of this medical alphabet soup are all the emotions that come with each stage of this journey to motherhood. And boy, isn't it a journey? I wanted to approach this very hard thing in a way that made me a better person, a better woman. I believe a journey can leave its mark on you, or you can leave your mark along the way. Here is how I have been traversing this path.

The feeling of failure at what is usually seen as a natural thing was oppressive — a weight that hung on me like a heavy coat.

Was I being punished because I had not always wanted children? Will my husband still love me even if we cannot have our own children despite interventions? Am I even a real woman? What if I am not meant to have children at all and this is a clear sign? What if I force the issue and it goes horribly wrong?

It was a season mired in fear of the unknown, shame. Once my husband assured me of his love and continued support no matter the outcome, I reassessed what this could look like. I am prone to anxiety, but I did not want to let it rule the trajectory of my life. I paused and took stock of my life — what I wanted it to look like and represent. And I did what any good hospice social worker would do — I imagined myself on my deathbed and did a self-assessment.

As a person of (Christian) faith, I want my life to be about more than just me. *Is my sole purpose in life to have children, to be a mother?* I did not think so. It was a desire, but not a necessity. *If I never have children, am I still a worthy and already fulfilled human being?* Yes. *If I never have the title "mother," would that make me less of a woman in the eyes of God and my husband?* No.

I found peace in this assessment, and it shaped the way for how the rest of my journey would unfold. I found the glory in my story. I tried to view my journey akin to the way I imagine a miner sees a mine quarry or an oil prospector assesses a flat piece of land. On the surface and to the naked eye, one is not aware of the gems and valuables that will be unearthed. It will be messy, sometimes downright dangerous, work but I was ready for the challenge. I chipped away at myself to find what I hoped would be strength, resilience, and the wherewithal to endure what was to come.

The first thing I did was fight the urge to hide away in shame and give power to silent suffering. Here is where I found my first precious thing: sisterhood, otherwise known as "the village." I called upon the community of women I had surrounded myself with throughout my life. My sister, college girlfriends, women I met in church, my colleagues, and my family social group. I started an email with those women as willing or unwilling recipients, and I told them about this upcoming season in my life, sparing them no details over many months. This was an eclectic group of women who knew me in different capacities but were about to see this side of me as a group. They got used to my rhythm, saw more of my faith *and* my potty mouth, moments when I was full of hope and other times when I was angry, terrified, and filled with doubt. I had no expectations of them, save for an outlet into which I poured my struggles. They became my sister-warriors and my cheerleaders. They spoke truth and comfort into me when I could not muster those things on my own. They lamented with me when things did not go according to plan and oh, how they rejoiced when it was time to rejoice. I saw the power of women and friendship like never before, and I am proud to call these women my friends, my sisters.

As I got into the thick of things, where injections were part of the intervention, I once again reached outside myself. I worked with nurses during my first and second round of IVF, and I shared my journey with these co-workers. I would ask a nurse to give me a shot every day when I went to work (my poor husband had the weekend shift). It was a humbling experience to rely on these women to take time from the dying to help me start a new life. It was also humbling to show them my butt (and sometimes granny panties) five days a week. This was an opportunity to talk about infertility and to (literally) expose myself to their judgments and opinions. It was my chance to maybe be the one person they knew who did not want to perpetuate the societal and Hollywood version of assisted reproduction. To this day, I still think of them as having a hand in my daughter's life.

Can I be honest? Once I got to the twelve-week gestation mark and was released from my fertility doctor to my regular obstetrician (OB), I thought I deserved a break and a "normal" pregnancy from here on out. *Had I not suffered enough from being poked like a pincushion daily for months on end? Was it not sufficient to acquire new undies because I had ruined so many with aquamarine-coloured vaginal suppositories and blood, my lumpy butt squirting as the scar tissue resisted yet another needle stick?*

You know what helped me carry on when I felt like I was scaling a sheer rock face the likes of El Capitan? When my baby measured small, when I had a delivery that resulted in a four-degree tear and going home with a catheter, when my newborn wouldn't sleep without being held, or when I was told her skull may be fusing too quickly? Each new challenge felt like someone prying my fingers away from the cliff's edge. I felt unhinged every time, but the shared stories of my community of women gave me a net to catch me before I went *splat!* I would send a desperate text, and they would respond.

That was the next precious thing. *Those* responses meant they had to share their stories with me, their hardships, and their struggles. Those shared experiences helped keep me sane when I was drowning in the newness of motherhood, hormones, and sleep deprivation. Stories of overcoming an obstacle, even barely, kept me going. Even the ones in which a mama admitted her absolute failure at something made me feel better. The very thought of how different my IVF and early motherhood journey would have been had I not risked fear and embarrassment and mustered the courage to reach out to friends to share my experiences — good, bad, and ugly — makes me shudder. I was surviving on the glory of *their* stories when I could only see the gory in mine.

During my current pregnancy at the structural ultrasound, the doctor came in with the ultrasound nurse. In the moment, it was a little funny because I had asked the nurse if she had a practiced poker face for when things did not look right; she responded that she hoped she did and that the doctor has to deliver any bad news anyway.

Seriously, Nia, you just had to ask her that, didn't you?

The doctor then said she saw two soft markers for Down Syndrome. She went over the options for tests as I smiled and nodded, thinking how I would be late for my Thai lunch date. Before the door even closed behind me, I had texted my dear friend whose daughter has Down Syndrome. I have followed her incredible story from the beginning, and the power of it practically carried me down the two flights of stairs and through my lunch date until I could talk to my husband in person. I was not freaking out only because she shared her story in such an honest way. If she had kept her story and journey to herself, my story would look different right this minute.

The lesson: There is power in sharing your stories and messages, there is power and energy in shared sisterhood. I don't know how this story will unfold for me, but through my friend's story, I have a template for how it *could* unfold. You know the naked-in-front-of-the-entire-school dream? Imagine if someone or a few people joined you in that nakedness? You would no longer feel *as* alone in your embarrassment. In fact, you'd all have a good laugh and a shared experience for life. Her bravery became mine. Her exposure, if you will, became my cloak of comfort. *That* is the power of sharing your struggles, your victories, and your failures — there's power in those, too!

When I want to complain about some typical parental plight, I am reminded that this is what I signed up for. Don't get me wrong — I still gripe and complain about a failed naptime, but there is something in it that feels victorious. How miraculous is it that our daughter is here to keep us awake when she is teething! *This* is what I signed up for — the glory in the gory, day-to-day, amusement-park-meets-battleground that is motherhood. The glamour in the clamor! Each appointment, shot, pill, blood draw, and ultrasound all culminated in this darling child.

If you are in the throes of infertility, I hope with all my heart that it results in a precious child. It can be a long and harrowing journey from where you are now. Your platform doesn't have to be a lofty stage if and when the journey is victorious. It can be found in the trenches when you get a negative test, when your insurance doesn't cover jack diddly, when you get yet another baby shower invitation. The worthiness of your story is while it's happening.

Maybe it's not that misery loves company, per se; it's that we just need to see our pain reflected in someone else's story. A collective consciousness, an inspired, empowered, yet raw and honest sharing of our experiences as women, wives, mothers. There is no power in silent suffering or silent rejoicing. There is power in vulnerability; be the misery that company loves.

So look for the hidden gems along the way. You may discover them in yourself, your spouse, your friendships, or your faith. It is easy to keep your head down because IVF can be an all-consuming ordeal. But if you can lift your head up just long enough to look left or right, you will see another mama holding out her story, her suffering as a lifeline. And if you are the mama in the middle of her story or on the other side, consider sharing your journey, right now, right where you are. Unearth and display the gems you have mined from beneath the healed or still bleeding scars.

> ~ To those who have borne witness to my story and who have shared theirs, thank you. To the women who have stood with me, and stand with me still, thank you. To the most wonderful husband, our precious children, and the God who gives good gifts, thank you.

12

IT'S HARDER
THAN YOU THINK

by Meghan Krmpotic

"How do you say goodbye to someone you never had the chance to meet?"

Meghan Krmpotic

Born and raised in Ottawa, Ontario, Canada, Meghan has always been creative and passionate, a people-person who enjoyed television and the entertainment industry. Determined not to have a *boring* job, she moved to Toronto permanently and pursued a career in Canadian television production after university. This seemed like the perfect fit; working on several number one Canadian reality and lifestyle shows allowed her to travel across Canada, work with incredible people, and really fuel her creative drive and love for television. This career was an amazing place-holder until her true *dream job* came around: becoming a Mama.

For Meghan, once her first child was born, all her priorities changed. Her television career was no longer what fueled her passion. She loved her time at home with her kids more. Four years later, she could no longer ignore her gut feeling that there was more to her life than daycare pickups and cranky children. She made a career change that allows her more flexibility and time freedom. She is now a regional vice president with the health and wellness company Arbonne International and gets to spend the majority of her time empowering others and hanging out with her kiddos. This wife and mom of three understands the value of showing her children how to dream big and live a life by design and is committed to exactly that.

ig: @mekrmpotic
fb: Meghan Cavanagh Krmpotic
photo credit: @oliveandivyphotography

~To my tiny humans — Grace, Alexander, and Frankie, thank you for giving me my dream job. I am filled to the brim each day with the incredible love I have for each one of you. To my four little souls whom we lost, thank you for your lessons. There is a special place in my heart just for you. To my incredible husband, Daniel, without you none of this is possible. You are the rock our family is built upon. To my own mama, thank you for teaching me what unconditional love feels like. And for the heads up on how hard this job is!

"DESIRE backed by FAITH, pushed reason aside, and
inspired me to carry on."
~ Napoleon Hill

"It's harder than you think, Meghan . . ."

I remember my mother's gentle words of wisdom when I expressed my childhood desire to have a large family all too well. My childhood self could not imagine what could be so hard about this. I had two siblings but wished for more. In my childhood innocence, I obviously had no idea! I would save my allowance and buy wedding magazines. I would spend hours looking at those dresses and planning my fairy-tale wedding. Stacks of paper contained detailed drawings of my future family, always with at least three children. There was never any limit to how many children I wanted or any specific order or gender. It was fun to let my vivid imagination run free and know the possibilities were endless. As a child of divorce at the age of seven who lived through re-marriage and divorce again less than five years later, I craved stability, unity, and strength, which I would ensure by creating a strong future family unit to call my own.

To my current adult-parent-self, my mother's gentle warning makes so much sense now in hindsight. I now know EXACTLY what she meant. Being a mom is hard . . . really freaking hard. It's impossible to prepare anyone for things like the newborn zombie stage, sleepless nights, breastfeeding, projectile vomiting, poop explosions, fevers, constant worry, bedtime battles, picky eaters, potty-training, shuttling to activities, tantrums, hospital stays, broken bones, rice cleanup (this is the worst!), and raising good, loving, consciously aware kids in a scary world. All of those things are hard and will always be. Trust me, we are all on the battleground of raising kids, and nothing about it seems very easy except loving them and kissing them while they are fast asleep. We are just "momming hard," doing our best every day to raise good humans.

What I also didn't know as a child was just how hard it would be for me to fulfill my vision of that family. I did have the wedding of my dreams, and my amazing husband was aligned with my vision of many children. We were ready, and I thought it was going to be so easy.

Grace Elizabeth was born on February 6th, 2011 at 4:14am, nine days late after thirty-six hours of labor. This was after a fairly easy and uneventful nine months of pregnancy. We started "trying" for a baby the year after we got married. I put the word "trying" in quotation marks because my husband Daniel basically just looks at me and I am pregnant. To his dismay, not much "trying" has ever been needed for us. I am forever grateful that it is easy for us to conceive.

Of course, I had concerns: *What if I can't get pregnant right away? What if I can't get pregnant at all?* And then of course once I was pregnant: *What if I miscarry? Why don't I feel nauseous? Oh I'm so nauseous, when will this go away? Is that a kick? What if something is wrong with the baby? Uh-oh, now I have to deliver this baby, how do I do that?*

But all in all, I thoroughly enjoyed my pregnancy. We went on our merry way to discover the realities of having a newborn and subsequently a toddler. She didn't like to sleep and was super-active and strong-willed, but she was a piece of perfection in our eyes. I was enjoying my time off with her and although I wasn't ready to jump right into having another baby, the wheels in my head turned pretty quickly after she was born. It was time to plan when baby number two would make an appearance.

I was a little shocked when I found out I was pregnant with baby number two when Grace was fourteen months old. I had been planning for a full two-year age gap. I felt a bit overwhelmed because she was still so young, but I was also excited. I had none of the first-pregnancy jitters and started to plan for a Christmas baby.

When I started bleeding less than two weeks later, I didn't want to believe it was true. I knew miscarriage was something that affected fifteen to twenty percent of pregnancies, but because my pregnancy with Grace had been so smooth, I believed that I was invincible. That it would not and could not happen to me. It was crushing when the midwife called to confirm that the pregnancy was no longer viable. I was having a miscarriage. I was gutted, heartbroken, and could not get off the couch. I drank wine, ate takeout Thai food, devoured the cookie basket my friends had sent me, and cried . . . a lot.

Only my closest friends knew what had transpired, no one else. For some reason, I was ashamed to tell anyone else. My midwife recommended I take some time off work, as the fetus was passing naturally and it could be quite painful. I ignored those recommendations and didn't take one day off. I still went in, rushing to the bathroom hourly and crying as the remains of the pregnancy passed through me. I felt like my body had failed me. My brain could tell me how "common" this was and that most likely, the fetus had not been healthy, but logic provided little to no solace to my broken heart. I had already identified this baby as mine the moment I knew I was pregnant with him or her.

I picked myself up after dwelling in the loss for a few weeks and looked forward. *When could I start trying again?* One miscarriage would not hold me back from my dream of building a family. I was happily pregnant again within three months. Cautiously optimistic and hopeful, I was excited again. Three weeks into the pregnancy, that blood reared its ugly head again. My stomach dropped — not again!

I rushed myself into an ultrasound and right away, the technician showed me a strong heartbeat. I wanted to jump up and kiss her. I had a subchorionic hematoma, which was the cause of the bleeding. I was told not to worry, as most women carry on with healthy pregnancies and the hematoma gets absorbed. I would just have to get used to the blood because spotting would continue until it went away.

This was something I could never wrap my head around. To me, blood was a sign of loss, so how could I carry on and not worry about it? My stomach was in knots every time I went to the bathroom, and the worry never went away. One month later, I was in Calgary for work and I could not ignore the bleeding any longer.

My midwife ordered me straight to the emergency room after hearing how many pads I was soaking through in an hour. I had to take myself there in a cab, bawling my eyes out and hemorrhaging blood. I was rushed into a room, seen almost immediately, and sent up to surgery for an emergency dilation and curettage (D&C). I was all alone; my husband was home with our daughter and could not get a flight until the next morning. I was even more · broken. *How much more could I endure?*

But I picked myself back up again because I had no choice. I had a daughter who needed me. We went to a wedding that weekend because *life goes on.* Again, I suffered in silence, feeling all alone because I couldn't and *didn't* want to share my experience with anyone. I gave myself a few more months to heal, but truly, those months seemed to last forever. All I wanted was another baby.

Less than six months later, we were pregnant again, and although I was nervous, I believed I had paid my dues. I did not think any more loss could come my way in this department because I could not bear it.

Seven weeks into the pregnancy, and again, the dreaded "spotting." To my complete and utter shock, I learned I was pregnant with twins. Unfortunately, the midwife called later with the not-so-good news. The bleeding was most likely because one twin was passing. The heartbeat was not great, and it was much smaller than the other. This was confirmed within a week. I was upset about this loss but focused on finding gratitude for the one baby with a heartbeat who was still growing within me and counting on me as his or her mama.

From that point on, though, my pregnancy experience was marred; I felt uneasy. Even when it got past the twelve-week gestation mark, there was something in my gut that didn't feel right. I didn't really want to tell people, but it got to the point when I couldn't hide it anymore.

By sixteen weeks, there was kicking, movement, and the heartbeat was always strong. I had so much anxiety around this pregnancy that I would rush myself to an ultrasound almost every week. Just shy of twenty weeks, I had intense cramping and more spotting. Back to ultrasound I went just for *peace of mind*, not wanting to bother my husband to come with me again. It was there, sitting in that dark room and NOT having the technician show me a heartbeat right away, that I knew this baby was no longer alive. Tears were streaming down my face. I was escorted into a small office and the midwife confirmed what I knew in my heart — there was no longer a heartbeat.

I couldn't breathe. I looked down at my big belly and could not process how something that was just kicking me the week before was gone. *My baby, this new life that was growing inside me, kicking me, developing his or her personality in my womb, was now still, lifeless. How could my body betray me once again? How much more loss could one woman, one mother possibly endure?*

What followed next were the worst twenty-four hours of my life. It felt like hell on high speed — an overwhelming myriad of emotions, physical, mental, emotional pain, and an unshakeable emptiness.

I wanted this to be a nightmare I would soon wake up from. Being induced to deliver a baby who would never live to see daylight, feel my touch or kisses, hear my voice, or know his or her sister and father. Having severe hallucinations as a result of being on high doses of pain medication. Getting up to go to the bathroom and having the baby drop out of me into the toilet. Not being brave enough to even look at the baby or find out if it was a boy or a girl. Because the baby was just under twenty weeks, it was considered just another miscarriage in medical terms. However, to us, it was so much more.

How do you say goodbye to someone you never got the chance to know in the first place?

I just wanted everything to be over and done with, erased completely, like it never happened. Except everyone in my life knew about it this time. There was no more hiding. People want to be there for you, but they don't know what to say. Everyone wants an answer as to why this has happened, but you don't have it. I didn't want to see a pregnant woman or talk to any of my pregnant friends. My husband was supportive, but he didn't carry the same emotional and physical scars that I did. My anger was palpable. It was stronger than my sadness. Then followed a surge of guilt for feeling so angry. I went to therapy. I finally forgave myself for not being brave and for all the negative feelings I had about myself and others.

Throughout this time, I felt like I would never have another baby. I looked to friends who had fertility struggles and thought that maybe I should just be grateful to even have my firstborn. But in my heart, I knew one was not enough for me. I knew even at my lowest point that I would persevere until I had the family I had dreamed about as a child. I would make my vision come true even if I couldn't conceive again. It's true when they say what doesn't kill you makes you stronger. I never thought I could bear more than what I did with my second miscarriage, but I ended up going through much worse.

I went to see a specialist for recurrent miscarriages. Under careful watch from her, we conceived naturally. My fifth pregnancy was monitored closely and was fairly uneventful — except gone were the days of excitement and elation. That version of myself had disappeared, and I mourned her greatly. Anxiety and stress were with me every time I went to the bathroom; these were the longest nine months of my life.

Our son Alexander Paul was born on May 26, 2014, just one year and three days after delivering that baby without a heartbeat. Twenty-three months later, our youngest daughter, Frances Katharine, was born without any complications in between. My eldest daughter was finally a sister, and I had the babies I knew I was meant to have.

While I was living through those two years of being pregnant and not pregnant, it felt like an eternity. Now it feels like it was a lifetime ago. It's amazing how something can be all-consuming when you're in it — like a never-ending drought, an endless famine, with no light in sight, and five years later, seems like a blip on your parenting journey radar, especially as you are knee-deep in the daily struggles of parenting three children under the age of five.

What brought me great solace during my two-year struggle to add to our family were stories of success. I would spend hours scouring the internet, looking for blogs and stories of women who had multiple miscarriages and still went on to have successful pregnancies. I had a phone conversation with a friend I had not seen since high school just because she had a similar story. I will admit, it became somewhat of an obsession. I wanted to prove that the odds were in my favour. I had to know how these women could bear these losses and still carry on. I had to know it was possible, and that I was not alone. "Rainbow baby" became one of my top Google searches.

I would cling to these stories as my only truth, my only possibility, and they helped me keep fighting for my rainbow baby. I discovered some journeys that seemed way worse than mine — five, six, seven miscarriages, some who had stillborn babies, and some who lost infants right after they were born. I also found stories of joy, perspective, strength, and, most of all, hope. These stories helped me keep my vision alive.

I also felt a strong sense of responsibility to share my story as a means of providing others with the same solace and hope I found through these years. Without desire, vision, and faith, I could not have carried on. Without other mamas expressing bravery and putting their stories out there, I would not have found my inner strength.

Miscarriage is a topic, a dialogue, a discourse that needs to be had, a conversation that needs to come to light and stay open instead of hiding behind the stigma and tabooed connotations associated with it. This can only happen when we are brave enough to talk about it, to share that it has happened to us. You are *not* any less of a woman, a mother, or a human being or any less beautiful because you endured a miscarriage. Everyone is so sorry and sad to hear it; yet nobody wants to talk about it boldly, unashamed, even though their mom, aunt, best friend, cousin, sister has experienced it, too. We rarely ever talk about the physical and emotional pain that miscarriage carries. We almost never talk about the gory details, the gut-wrenching feeling of dread, the extreme blood, the horrible pain. It's as if those of us who have gone through it gain membership to a secret club and the graphic details are an unspoken bond that needs no further explanation. My hope is that we can start to normalize this conversation since so many of us have suffered these losses. For those who have not, you, too, can link arms and truly empathize.

Would I change what happened on my journey to complete my family? Would I have wanted less blood, less loss, less emptiness, less pain?

Had you asked me these questions five years ago, I would have said yes, absolutely, please make this all stop. But ask me now, and I would say absolutely not. I would not change a single thing. And not because I now have three healthy children. Every tear shed, every child mourned, every due date passed, all the anxiety I endured and the anger I released is what steered the course of who I am now, the kind of mother I am, and the decisions I have made for me and my family. With every hardship comes strength. Difficulty breeds persistence. There is always a lesson to be learned. After every dark cloud comes a rainbow.

I learned what I was made of and discovered I could endure much more loss than I thought I ever could. I learned that my desire and vision for the family I wanted was enough to make my childhood dreams come true. I have learned to surrender to aligned or Divine timing instead of drill-sergeant family planning, because really, you cannot control any of it. I learned that even though I prayed every night for that healthy baby and made bargains with God such as, *"In exchange for this, I would never take the baby for granted, get frustrated with him or her, and always be the 'perfect, happy, and doting' mother,"* this was a promise I cannot humanly keep. The best part? It is okay! It really is!

I learned that even though I felt like I wanted this baby more than anyone else in the world and had to go through the depths of despair to get it, at the end of the day, we are still just human beings. The baby is still going to have colic, scream for hours on end in the car, and throw epic tantrums. Why? Because unfortunately babies and toddlers have not received the memo that we worked really hard to bring them here. Because they are babies, they are a blank slate, pure and innocent, looking to their mamas and dadas to guide them and, most of all, love them for everything they are. They are just babies and toddlers, period, and they will do what babies and toddlers do. I learned it is okay to still be frustrated, exhausted, and hormonal and to still hate nighttime feedings. None of this takes away from the fact that you wanted this baby, that you love this child, and that this tiny human was meant for your family.

People like to ask me now if our family is complete. When is baby number four coming? And the truth is, I don't know. What I do know is this: I am one hundred percent happy — three children or more. I am one hundred percent happy because I have the family that was destined for me. My experience has given me so much perspective. I now know not to get attached to any plan when it comes to building a family . . . sometimes there is a bigger and better purpose out there waiting for you to step into. I look at my three tiny humans and can't imagine life without those faces. With the loss of four little souls, I've also gained three bright ones who light me up daily.

13

LESSONS IN LOSS

by Taelar Howe

"Something we need to remember is, loss always carries with it a lesson."

Taelar Howe

Taelar is known for being a positive, outgoing soul. She knew from a young age that she wanted to help and inspire people around her. As her mom would tell you, she always had a knack for figuring out why something didn't work. By the time she was twenty-four years old, she had already dabbled in hairstyling, jewelry-making, writing, blogging, furniture-building, and much more. She became a mother to her son, Axell James Howe, in November 2017. A lot of her dreams changed that day, from wanting to own a small home decor business to helping moms throughout their motherhood journey. Finally finding a way to help and inspire others, Taelar created an online community, *Howe Moms Do It*, for mothers at any stage to share, vent, learn, teach, and empower one another, which she shares publicly on her Instagram account. When she isn't creating, you can find her getting lost in her search for seaglass at her favorite beaches in California.

ig: @howemomsdoit
fb: HoweMDI

"Grief is like the ocean; It comes in waves. Ebbing and flowing. Sometimes the water is calm, and sometimes overwhelming. All we can do is learn to swim."
~ Vicki Harrison

When I was asked to contribute a chapter in this book to share my journey, I was full of joy. It was a dream come true; however, I was also filled with fear. *What will people think of my story? Will I be judged? Will someone change their opinion of me because of my choices?*

These thoughts have been running through my overstimulated brain ever since we received terrible news on September 21, 2016. Fear is such a full-body experience, and it's something I face daily — whether it be fear of loss, fear of failing, fear of not being good enough, or fear of something bad happening to my child or husband. It's funny how being a mom creates a new level of worry and stress in our worlds. Even if you have someone to watch your children for a few hours to get some "you time" or relaxation, you still cannot help but worry. It's how we are wired as moms. The entire time we have to ourselves, we have thoughts running rampant around every possible thing that could potentially go wrong with our baby — if they're sleeping enough, having regular bowel movements, eating well enough, choking on the next object they are curiously teething on, the list is endless. Let's face it, motherhood is beautiful, but full of constant worry. Sharing my story has helped me face my fears and overcome them, and my wish for you as you continue to read this beautiful book with raw, empowering stories of motherhood is to find that same hope and courage to face your fears as well!

Every mom knows that once they make their "birth-plan" to deliver that baby, nothing goes according to that plan! My journey to motherhood definitely didn't go according to plan. It all started when I was diagnosed with Polycystic Ovarian Syndrome (PCOS) six years ago. Growing up, I never had much of a menstrual cycle; my period was non-existent. As a teenage girl, it felt like I won the period lottery because most girls complained about their periods, the cramping, the mood swings, the junk food cravings, you name it. Yet I never thought too much of it. I didn't believe there was an underlying cause to my irregular, almost non-existent menstrual cycle.

This perspective changed when I nearly keeled over due to severe cramping, which led me straight to my obstetrician's office to have it examined. I thought I might have to change my birth control prescriptions and try a different brand instead. I'm sure you already have an idea of where I'm going with this story. My obstetrician found forty (yes, you're reading this correctly) small cysts on each ovary. I was told I had PCOS and that my chances of having a baby were slim to none. I felt like the someone just punched me in the gut. To say I felt shocked would be an understatement. I left there feeling a whirlwind of emotions. When I researched more on my diagnosis, I discovered the following: [2]

- Polycystic Ovarian Syndrome (PCOS) is a health condition that affects about ten million women around the world.
- There are three main factors that contribute to PCOS. The first is androgens. Androgens are referred to as the male hormone, but all women make androgens. Women with PCOS often have high levels of androgens, which are mostly produced by the ovaries and sometimes adrenal glands.
- The second factor is insulin, which allows the body to absorb glucose into the cells for energy. In the case of PCOS, the body isn't as responsive to insulin as it should be. This leads to elevated blood

2   Azziz, R., MD, MPH, & Ehrmann, D., MD (Eds.). (n.d.). Polycystic Ovary Syndrome (PCOS). Retrieved from https://www.hormone.org/diseases-and-conditions/womens-health/polycystic-ovary-syndrome

sugar levels and causes the body to make more androgens. -The last thing is the lack of progesterone, which leads to irregular periods. PCOS is the leading cause of infertility and complications during pregnancy.

That very day, I chose to stop taking birth control pills and let my body get back to its natural rhythm and state.

About four years later, I started to feel those same cramps again. This time, being a little older and more aware, I chose to take a more natural approach and instead of taking synthetic hormones to regulate my periods or balance my symptoms, I changed my diet and started acupuncture treatments on a regular basis. Boy, did that work! I'd feel lighter, relaxed, and more balanced with each treatment — hormonally and, of course physically. Two weeks later, my boobs started to grow, which was awesome, *I mean, come on, free boob job anyone?*

Anyone who has been pregnant knows where this is going.

A pregnancy never crossed my mind because of my PCOS diagnosis — I was told my chances of conceiving a child naturally were very slim. My boyfriend at the time (now husband) mentioned how big my boobs were getting. He kept making jokes about me being pregnant and I just kept blowing it off.

Me, pregnant? Couldn't be.

Then the raging hormonal emotions set in. It was like my body was on an emotional rollercoaster every minute; I felt like I was spiraling out of control. One minute I was crying, the next I was overjoyed. I had never felt like this before — something was different. The very next week, I took three pregnancy tests. Sure enough, he was right — all of them said "pregnant."

So many thoughts were going through my mind. *What will my parents think? What will everyone else think? We aren't married! Where will we live?*

A big lesson I had learned after this was to not care what anyone else thought. And that is also one of the biggest lessons in motherhood. I'm sure almost everyone, at some point, has done something, instantly thought, *I wonder what other people will think,* and forgot about why they chose to do it in the first place. We make a lot of decisions based on feeling, intuition, and emotion.

Every chapter you will read in this book is written by mothers who have gone through something they didn't plan. A lot of us envision perfection and are let down when things don't go a certain way. It can be challenging to change our perfectionist mindset, and we are often left disappointed because of it.

Let me tell you now, from experience: I have learned you have no control over your birth experience. From the moment I knew I was pregnant, everything changed. I instantly felt every pregnancy symptom. It seemed like the very next week, I felt what us mamas know as morning sickness. Boy, did it kick me on my ass and never stop. They say morning sickness, but for me, it was more like four months of non-stop throwing up and hourly visits with my new best friend, Mr. Toilet!

I hit twenty-one weeks and we were able to find out the baby's gender. We were so excited to learn it was a girl! The ultrasound technician just needed to perform the second anatomy scan, and we were confident that everything would be perfect, just as it was at the fourteen-week scan. He said he needed a better scan of her heart and brought me some juice to drink. He said the sugars would get the baby moving, that she was in a weird position. I thought that was a little strange but brushed it off because I was just so excited about our baby girl.

That very next moment changed our lives forever. After another twenty minutes of scanning, the ultrasound technician left the room again. He returned with two ladies this time; they congratulated us on the gender and let us know they had found something in the scan they wanted to get a better look at. My husband and I both looked at each other and instantly knew something was not right. They wanted us to make an appointment at Stanford Hospital the next day to meet with a heart specialist.

We left there with a very different feeling than we had walking in. We got our ultrasound images, which ironically had an image in which the baby had her thumb up. Call it superstition or blind faith, but the eternal optimist in me felt as though she was telling us it would be okay. The next day we headed to Stanford Hospital and met with the cardiovascular specialist. There we had another ultrasound; this time it took about two hours because the baby was still in a weird position and wasn't really moving. They finally finished and took us to this office room to tell us the results of our ultrasound.

I entered the room feeling confident, like everything was okay, probably because of the thumbs-up sign we saw in our ultrasound image yesterday. The doctor informed us that they had found a congenital heart defect during the ultrasound. The baby had Hypoplastic Left Heart Syndrome (HLHS) and was missing the main aortic valve. This means the left side of the heart is smaller than the right side. The left side pumps blood to the brain and major organs, while the right side pumps mainly to the lungs. This heart defect affects two to three percent of every ten thousand babies born with a heart defect.

The doctors also informed us that with the aortic valve missing, the chances of her being born still (meaning not alive) were high. If she did survive the birth, she would have to have open heart surgery immediately, and three more to follow by the time she was four years of age. We were given two options to choose from in less than twenty-four hours because in the state of California, you can no longer terminate a pregnancy after twenty-four weeks.

This isn't happening right now. Someone, anyone, please wake me up from this nightmare!

Option one: We could continue the pregnancy and hope she lived through the birth to have her first open heart surgery. Option two: Choose an elective termination. We were sent home with little research and a time limit on our life-or-death decision for our daughter. Talk about feeling completely out of control and hopeless.

This moment changed everything for us. The bright-eyed, hopeful, young and unstoppable egos left us. We instantly became adults when we experienced firsthand that life can change in a matter of seconds; at any given moment, death was just a moment away, whether we liked it or not. How could we even think about making a decision in twenty-four hours with the news we just received? I couldn't think about anything, and I felt nothing but anger and questioning. *Why us?*

We went home and tried to research as much as possible. All that kept coming up were videos and pictures of HLHS babies connected to tubes with incision marks on their chest from multiple open heart surgeries. Most of these were mild cases; our baby had a missing valve that they would have to construct. I instantly became sick to my stomach and couldn't bear to research anymore. What happened next was the hardest moment in my life, the toughest and most heartbreaking decision I ever had to make. The feeling of confusion, of uncertainty, of not knowing the right answer haunted me. If only someone could just tell us what to do.

We had to go back to the hospital to get one last ultrasound to double-check and confirm the doctor's findings, in case the baby had moved and they could get a better look at the heart. As I laid down for the ultrasound, I remembered the thumbs-up we got a few days earlier from her. I couldn't do anything but close my eyes and see her little fingers. It felt like she was guiding me and letting us know that whatever we choose, it would all be okay. The last few days replayed in my mind; anger, sadness, frustration, and immense hurt had taken over my body. But in that moment, with my eyes closed, I could think more clearly than ever before in my life. It was as if this little baby had taken all my pain, hurt, and anger and given me the courage to do what I truly felt was right despite the fear and grief. I knew our path was to take control and choose what I thought was the best thing for this little baby.

We now have a guardian angel watching over us in heaven. As a mom, I couldn't feel more confident in the decision we chose for her.

Nothing can ever prepare you for what loss will bring you. It leaves you feeling empty and confused. *How could something like this happen to us?* What we didn't know then was that this was a life lesson. We could choose either to stay mad and angry or to learn from this and grow. You're put in these types of situations to re-evaluate both yourself and your life. Life has a funny way of doing that.

If you're going through a loss or a grieving period, talk about it! That is the healthiest way to cope. Talk to someone, share your story, and don't be scared or ashamed. I remember thinking, *I don't want to see anyone, I am sure they will ask what happened.* I was scared to be judged or shamed for our choice. But in actuality, it didn't matter what anyone else thought — they weren't living our life. They did not know even an ounce of the pain we felt, the sadness that plagued us when we found out our baby girl was given two options: have a barely-there chance to live a life or to die before you're even fully born. No, they had absolutely no idea what we went through.

Discovering that what other people think is none of my business has been the biggest life lesson yet. As a result of this lesson, I feel less stressed and am more able to live in the moment. Caring less about what others think lets you be present in the moment and choose with your heart and intuition, not with clouded judgment or scattered emotions. Something we need to remember is that loss always carries with it a life lesson. You just have to find what that lesson is.

I learned to never take any day for granted. You never know when your last day will be. To never judge anyone; you may never really know what they are going through. To trust my motherly instincts, because most of the time they are right. In times of struggle, to dig deep and grow from the situation. To not dwell on the bad and instead to approach the future in a positive way.

Although we lost an amazing angel, a year later on November 6, 2017, we were blessed with a beautiful baby boy. He is so healthy and happy; he teaches me new things every day. It's crazy how much a little human can teach you about yourself.

I guess what I'm trying to say is this: Life will never go as planned. We are all dealt our own set of cards from this great deck called life. What matters most is we learn from each blow, we grow through each obstacle, and we play to win at all times. The victory need not be monetary or monumental. Sometimes the victory lies in overcoming what you never thought you would or celebrating another life even though you lost a part of your heart when you lost your baby. You will still feel pain, but you will feel sheer joy as well. Never forget who you are as a person, and don't get lost in the little voices or petty opinions of others.

If you're dealing with loss, talk about it. Share your story, and you will be surprised by how many people you will meet with similar journeys. Sharing your story and expressing your feelings will give you strength and courage to heal, one step at a time, and will also inspire and guide others on their path to healing.

As we live our day-to-day life, we have never forgotten about the baby girl who started all of this for us. There are moments of *I wonder what she would've been like* and moments of sadness and forever grieving. I thank her for teaching me to be a better mom and wife and, most of all, a stronger and more understanding person for my family and friends.

~To my best friend and **amazingly** *supportive husband*
To my beautiful healthy son, Axell James Howe
To Baby Sterling, who will be with us forever

14

FOLLOW YOUR DREAMS, THEY KNOW THE WAY

by Justine Dowd

"Be kind and loving with yourself when you are struggling. Everyone's journey is unique."

Justine Dowd

Compassionate, genuine, and insightful, Justine is passionate about empowering others to heal themselves holistically. A dedicated researcher, she has always been fascinated by the psychology of behaviour change, which led her to complete a PhD in health psychology. Justine found an unexpected muse when she discovered she had celiac disease immediately before she began her doctoral studies. The diagnosis would not only influence her lifestyle but would shape her future. Justine focused her work on dietary behaviours and coping strategies for people living with celiac disease, which earned her a number of research awards early on in her career.

Justine made the connection between life experience and professional passion again after she and her husband struggled with "undiagnosed infertility" for over two years. During this time, Justine was inspired by the teachings of Kristen Neff and Brené Brown, from whom she learned about self-compassion and found the courage to be vulnerable. After fostering greater compassion for herself, Justine was motivated to help others do the same.

Justine's popular Gut Health Seminars and Holistic Fertility Retreats allow her to connect with kindred spirits. There she shares her personal experiences, scientific knowledge, and loving support to help others find natural solutions for their gut health and fertility challenges. When she's not spending time with her family, Justine enjoys wine and soulful conversations with an amazing group of women she's blessed to call friends. Justine lives in Calgary, Alberta, Canada with her husband, son, a second baby due December 2018, and furbaby, Callie.

www.justinedowd.com

ig: @justinedowd.phd | fb: @JustineDowdPhD

"There is no such thing as unexplained infertility,
just 'undiagnosed.'"
~ Dr. Geoffrey Sher, SIRM

I *'ve got this. I'm young, healthy, and married to my best friend. We've wait-*
ed until we are ready. Now all we have to do is start trying!

I defended my PhD in June 2014, so it made sense to me that I didn't get pregnant for the first few months. I was coming down off of a very stressful, busy, anxious time in my life. Defending my research — everything that I'd devoted my life to for over three and a half years — was understandably not the best time to get pregnant.

After six months of *still* not getting pregnant, though, I sought medical advice. My doctor ran a few tests and told me to relax, gain a few pounds on my 120-pound and five-foot-and-four-inch frame, and it would happen. Nevertheless, we proceeded to get a referral to the fertility clinic "just in case," fully believing we would cancel the appointment three months out from that date.

We started the full workup of fertility tests to get a head start on things — everything booked and prepped "just in case." Day three: blood work; day twenty-one: blood work. Temperature tracking, cervical mucus tracking, peeing on ovulation sticks. Repeat. Pregnancy tests. Negative pregnancy tests. Repeat grueling and nerve-wracking process all over again.

The next thing I knew, we were attending appointments and taking tests not to err on the side of caution but because we felt like we needed to. Days turned to weeks which then turned to months. What I thought was a temporary delay in our plans felt like a deeper hole being carved right within my stomach.

Soon it was a year since we started trying to conceive. Negative pregnancy test after negative pregnancy test. Tears. Heartache. Frustration. Confusion. Anger. Disappointment. At myself, my body, my essence as a woman. It was an extremely painful, invasive, and demoralizing experience — I felt like a lab rat undergoing every test from Hysterosalpingogram (HSG), a test for tubal infertility in which radioactive dye was shot into my uterus and fallopian tubes to ensure everything was clear, to weekly (if not daily) bloodwork and ultrasounds. Despite having the support of my husband and the wonderful nurses and doctors along the way, I began wondering, *What is wrong with me?*

All the tests came back "normal."

"Relax and it will happen!"

Um okay . . . But what is wrong with me?

Weekly acupuncture sessions. I focused on eating even healthier and exercised regularly. Meditation became my new best friend, along with yoga. Relax. Repeat routine. Repeat mantra: Relax — *it will happen.*

I found out my best friend was pregnant. *I'm happy for her . . . right? I should be thrilled I get to be an aunty to both of her adorable children!* Except all I can think about is how I am still not pregnant. My heart aches for a baby. To become a mama. *This is all I have ever wanted, and with every month that passes I keep getting more worried that it will never happen for me.* Tears and more tears.

Just have lots of sex! Then it will happen!" *they* said.

What is wrong with me? Maybe a vacation will help? Hawaii, here we come!

Still no luck. We came home to find out another good friend is pregnant. *Are you freaking kidding me?! I feel like I am going to lose my mind. It has now been eight months of "trying" with zero luck. I feel overwhelmed. I feel jealous and I resent her and never want to see her again. Why does she deserve to be a mama and I don't? What the hell is wrong with me? What is wrong with my body?*

Tears, heartache, and more tears.

Counseling.

What is wrong with me?

More negative pregnancy tests . . . More counseling.

Throughout our journey, I tried to embrace the practice of self-compassion. I study self-compassion. I have my PhD in health psychology. *I can do this! Wait — why can't I do this? What is going on? What is my body trying to tell me?*

I started reflecting back to my childhood and teenage years. For years as a teenager and young adult, I would have vivid dreams that I was pregnant. I would go into the hospital and they would say, "No, it's just gas." Weird, right? Intuition is a powerful thing. Once I was diagnosed with celiac disease in 2010, the dreams stopped. In hindsight, perhaps they were an early warning sign that issues with pregnancy could be related to my celiac disease. But how?

Then the new dreams started. Right after I would ovulate, I would dream that I was pregnant. Night after night, I felt in my heart that I was pregnant! Pregnancy tests were always negative, but my soul told me I was pregnant. Then a night or two before I was due to get my period, I would have vivid dreams that I was no longer pregnant. Then I would get my period.

Weird, right? I think not. These dreams meant something. I would only find out the meaning behind my dreams six years later on a trip to the United States.

In the meantime, I was bombarded with more pregnant friends. More people I never wanted to see again. *I could avoid them for life, right?* Baby showers. Baby talk. Tears. Girls' nights with pregnancy announcements. Pregnancy tests literally being thrown around like candy at girls' nights. *I can't handle this. I want to hide. I am so overwhelmed with frustration, anger, resentment, and jealousy. I don't want to see anyone. I don't want to socialize because I have to be as healthy as possible. I wish I was invisible. Why can't I just make this happen? What is wrong with me?*

One of the most difficult parts of my journey was that none of the doctors could give me a reason for our infertility struggles. It became maddening to be told everything was "normal" or "looked great" — so why wasn't I pregnant?

Social media was the worst. It felt like every day, babies were being born. Every post showcased families celebrating their beautiful little ones. I was angry. I was jealous. *That's it,* I decided. *I'm off social media.* This step really helped my mental well-being. However, I still did not get pregnant.

I just don't want to see anyone. I remember telling my wonderful husband to go out to parties with our friends without me. All I wanted to do was stay home and hibernate. *I don't want to see anyone.* All anyone ever talked about (or at least it felt like this to me) was who was pregnant. I remember being at a party and a (well-meaning) friend told me that I should just let loose and drink and then it would happen. It had been 548 days of trying at that time. I started sobbing and left the party. It was an awful night.

During this time, I was fortunate to be part of a year-long chakra journey. This course was so incredibly powerful and healing for me. It gave me so much strength to keep going on. Every angel card I drew told me to meditate. Meditation would help me find our answer. As frustrating as it was, it also gave me the belief that *I* would find the answer to our fertility struggles. I had to laugh every time I drew the exact same angel card with the word *meditate* from a deck of sixty cards. The wonderful, wise Universe was certainly looking out for me during one of the most difficult times of my life.

Throughout this journey, I was never very open to in-vitro fertilization (IVF). Every doctor told me I didn't need to do it, and I didn't think I needed to go that route to get pregnant. I was determined to explore every natural avenue first.

After two years of having zero success conceiving and spending thousands of dollars on tests, treatments, and supplements — over seventy-five acupuncture sessions at five different clinics in three cities, eighteen sessions with two naturopaths, fifteen plus different types of Chinese herb combinations to "balance my hormones," twelve gut healing intravenous therapy (IV) sessions, consultations with three different reproductive endocrinologists, three private hypnotherapy sessions, daily meditation and yoga; incredibly strict gluten-, dairy-, corn-, and egg-free diet for over one year (The Autoimmune Protocol), not drinking alcohol, going to bed early, a year-long chakra journey, twelve sessions with an osteopath, thousands of wasted dollars spent on functional medicine, more than six different supplements per day, monthly blood tests (a record of twenty-two vials of blood taken from five locations on my body - yikes!), and of course "not trying" — it hit me one night after getting my twenty-fifth period since we started trying: I was ready to do anything it took to get pregnant.

Don't get me wrong. I wholeheartedly believe in a holistic *natural* approach to fertility! While none of these things were the single "answer" for me, I know that everything I did helped me to get as healthy as possible for our next step. Not surprisingly, "just relax" wasn't all I had to do to get pregnant.

April 2016.

I'm at the end of my rope. How can I go on if I can't become a mama? Will this ever happen for me?

I was away at a conference in Seattle with my colleague. We were out for dinner with her brother and his kids. Watching this wonderful father interact with his beautiful kiddos, I had this surreal, out-of-body experience and knew in the depths of my being that I still had some push left in me. I would do everything I possibly could do to get pregnant. I absolutely did not want to be fifty years old and not have given my every shot to experience the magical opportunity of pregnancy, labour, and having my own babe.

But how do you keep going forward when nothing has worked for twenty-five cycles? When the test results show you are actually going backwards? I had to listen to my gut, my intuition, that voice within who whispered every day, "You are meant to be a mama, you'll find your way, mama." I just knew my time would come; I had to keep searching for the answer, and it would happen. My gut told we were missing something *key*. I guess this is where my stubborn, determined nature to persevere and get what *I want* in life really paid off.

It had been almost two years of trying. They say the definition of insanity is doing the same thing over and over again and expecting a different result. Well, it was finally time to try something new.

Sitting there at dinner with my colleague and her family, I just knew that I had to try IVF. IVF isn't the right choice, or even a feasible choice, for many people; however, in my heart, I knew it was the right choice for us to try next.

The next morning, I woke up and something struck me to research "autoimmune infertility." I swear I'd done this before at the start of our journey, but I purposely hadn't Googled much since then so that I could "relax and let it happen." Maybe it was timing or maybe it was being in the United States that influenced my Google search, but I think that it was finally time in my journey and that I was open to the answer. Perhaps surrendering to IVF, or surrendering to the pressure I had put on myself, allowed this moment to finally arrive.

I logged in to the hotel internet and typed '"autoimmune infertility" into the search engine on my iPhone.

Dr. Sher – haveababy.com – Infertility and Autoimmune Implantation Dysfunction was the number one hit.

OMG. What is this? My heart raced as I opened the link.

I read everything I could as fast as I could. *Oh my God! This might actually be our answer!* People with autoimmune diseases like celiac disease and Hashimoto's Hypothyroidism often have overly activated natural killer cells in their uterus that destroy the embryo every time it tries to implant.

Oh my God. This felt exactly like what was happening to me. Everything my dreams had been telling me — I would get pregnant and then my body would attack the embryo.

I immediately sent the link to my husband, mom, and best friend. "Look! I think this is what has been happening to me!" Everyone immediately agreed that it seemed to fit the bill.

We booked a Skype appointment with Dr. Sher for his earliest availability. After an amazing initial consult, we signed up right away for the next possible cycle, June 2016, laughing to ourselves that we would have to go to Las Vegas to get pregnant!

The next two months passed by quickly as we got all the necessary paperwork and pre-testing done. The testing recommended by Dr. Sher regarding autoimmune and alloimmune infertility all came back positive. Finally! We had discovered the root cause! Overactive natural killer cells in my uterus. My dreams were right all along. I was getting pregnant every month and then my body would attack the embryo. I started on the medications and every IVF supportive supplement pronto! We were getting ready to go to Vegas for eleven days. Finally, we felt confident that we had an answer.

Everything went as smoothly as possible in Las Vegas. My husband and I got to enjoy some quality time together, and lots of rest as well, which my body needed to do a fresh embryo transfer five days after egg retrieval. We went home and began the dreaded two-week wait. Wow, what a long two weeks. We ended up being out of town for a wedding when we had to go for the bloodwork to see if I was pregnant. The morning that we could go get the testing done, we raced into the closest town possible for the blood draw. That afternoon, when we were anxiously awaiting the call, we popped into a grocery store to pick up a few things. Unknowingly, my phone lost service in the store; when we were at the counter checking out, it beeped, indicating I had a missed voicemail. My husband was busy bagging our groceries when I clicked to listen to the call. I knew I should wait for him, but I just couldn't! He was shaking his head saying, "Wait," when I was listening to the message.

"Hi Justine — it's Briana. Your beta human chorionic gonadotropin (HCG) blood test results are in — your first value was 105 and the one today was 262 — so you are officially good and pregnant!"

My eyes went wide in shock and the biggest grin took over my face. My husband knew it was good news. We ran out of the grocery store and celebrated our news in the parking lot. I jumped into his arms and we danced around like two crazy people by our car. Wow, we were finally pregnant! We were totally overcome with joy — all of our crazy efforts finally paid off.

Two and a half weeks later, I was able to have the first early dating ultrasound. We went into the room, the ultrasound began, and the tech said, "See that right there? That's your baby's heartbeat! Perfectly healthy."

WOW! Could it be true? A huge step in the right direction! We knew that we still had a long way to go and a lot of things could go wrong before we could truly celebrate our baby growing inside of me. *More waiting. Painful waiting.* My daily meditation practice and faith in my journey — my intuition that our son would be healthy — helped me get through that first trimester.

A few weeks later, our twelve-week scan went well — all clear! However, Dr. Sher had recommended that we do further testing, an amniocentesis, at sixteen weeks, so we still had to wait another four weeks for this test. We celebrated each little step in the right direction, but the numerous appointments and tests were weighing on us. *When can we actually just celebrate and enjoy being pregnant?* The weeks leading up to the amniocentesis were very emotional. As much as I thought I could just be happy that I was pregnant, there was so much doubt circling within my mind about whether or not things would be okay. I continued to feign happiness for other people with healthy, uncomplicated pregnancies.

Fortunately, the amniocentesis went as well as possible. Then we had to wait. *Again.* The nurses said it could be anywhere from one to three weeks until the results were ready. One week later, the fateful phone call came in when I was driving by myself. The nurse said, "I have great news for you, the results are normal. You officially have a regular risk pregnancy." Finally, we could celebrate!

It was a weird feeling to finally be able to share our wonderful news with our loved ones. Even though I'd had three ultrasounds showing a beautiful, kicking babe, I just couldn't bring myself to say the words, "I'm pregnant." So many emotions were tied up in those words. Anger and resentment of other women who had told me and hurt me (unintentionally!), the fear we lived with for the first sixteen weeks of this pregnancy, and then the unknown. What if it wasn't okay? Even though the amniocentesis was "normal," we became aware that you are never truly in the clear with pregnancy or children. Something can always happen, and you can't control it.

This is where my faith in our journey was instrumental in coping. We had to just take it day by day, celebrate the little joys, and be grateful for everything we had been blessed with.

As I write the first version of this chapter, it is February 14, 2018, two days before my son's first birthday. Wow. I've been a mom for 363 days. I still cannot shake off my smile, and my heart cannot help but love on this little man.

I am so lucky and grateful to be a mama. Every stage with my son is more fun (and brings its own challenges!). Newborn snuggles were incredible. His amazing baby smell, his soft hair and smooth skin, his tiny, tender toes and hands, his cooing, and him nestling right into me when I held him in my arms. I've never been able to "just be" like that before — hours going by just holding my son, skin to skin. Developing a beautiful bond that we will share for a lifetime. Being a part of his development, watching him learn to hold his head up, make eye contact, smile, roll over, sit up, crawl, walk, talk, brush his teeth, and gently pet our dog. Getting to know his hilarious personality. Watching my husband become a father — the beautiful bond that he and my son share. Being a mama is better than I ever imagined it could be.

Motherhood is full of love and laughter, more rewarding and fulfilling than anything else I've ever done, yet also more challenging than anything I've taken on. The health scares, sleepless nights, temper tantrums, sleep training, feeding, and learning to let go. However, I wouldn't change any second of my journey. I have found peace with my struggles, knowing I went through everything that I did so that I can truly empathize with others who are there, too. Going through my struggles showed me how I can use my background in health psychology and my experiences with holistic health to empower other women to embrace their journey, find their answers, and fulfill their dreams to become mamas — in whatever capacity that means for them.

I want to express my wholehearted gratitude to the Universe for teaching me everything it did about patience and faith. Self-care. Self-love. Setting boundaries. Working through tough times with my husband. Falling even more in love with him as he was there for me in ways I never thought possible. Surrounding me with a loving, supportive health care team and friends who believed in us and our desire to get pregnant. Trusting in *our* journey. Trusting the process and knowing that everyone's is different. Helping me to give myself time to be in solitude when I needed it. Being patient and compassionate with myself.

If there are any words of wisdom I can leave you with at this point in my journey, they would be: **Be kind and loving with yourself when you are struggling, and be an advocate for yourself**. Everyone's journey is unique. While IVF in the United States was the right choice for us, there are numerous avenues one can go down to become a mother. Trust your gut, pay attention to your body, and never doubt yourself or your journey. You've got this, Mama!

~To my incredible husband, Lee: I wouldn't be where I am today without your unwavering love and support. To Liam, thank you for choosing me to be your mama; you have brought more joy into my life than I ever could have imagined. To all the supportive women and health care providers who helped me get to the other side of the biggest mountain I have ever climbed — thank you from the bottom of my heart.

15

FINDING MAGIC IN MADNESS

by Danielle Williams

"I've come to realize
life has many phases,
and death is just
one of them."

Danielle Williams

Danielle had an idyllic childhood attributable to small towns, big dreams, and the best family in the world. From a young age, she put pen to paper and was the recipient of many young author awards. After university, Danielle began a career in personal finance and made her best decision yet — marrying the love of her life, Russ. Though she has travelled much of the world, her heart remains firmly planted in the foothills of Alberta, Canada.

After the loss of their firstborn, Roark, Danielle began writing more extensively, becoming a self-proclaimed "grief student." This is her first in-print writing venture. You can find her personal musings and writing on Instagram. Danielle and Russ are the lucky parents of fiery Sterling Sophie, Roark, and Ellie (among the angels with Roark). They are filled with gratitude and joy to have recently welcomed another daughter, Bronwen, in October 2018.

Danielle is an entrepreneur at heart and an avid early riser, coffee drinker, and spirit junkie. She believes that there are gifts in all trauma — our goal is to find them and then share them with the world.

www.griefgratitudegrace.ca
ig: @danielle.g.w

"If you must look back — do so forgivingly. If you must look forward — do so prayerfully. However, the wisest thing you can do is to be present in the present, gratefully."
~ Maya Angelou

LOVE BEGETS LOVE
No more suffering. All of our love. Forever.
We are trapped in a sea of emotion.

On Saturday, July 19, at 5:40pm, on his twenty-third day of fighting, our little lion man, Roark, passed away in his daddy's arms. As he took his final breath, I held his hand and we kissed his head and whispered to him, "No more suffering." We promised. All of our love. Forever.

No child should spend their entire life in an incubator with breathing tubes, IV lines, blood draws, ultrasounds, and x-rays determining their every breath. And no parent should ever feel their child leave this earth.

But life isn't fair. Bad things happen to good people, and good things happen to good people. And we didn't deserve this. And we didn't get it handed to us because we can handle it. And it wasn't meant to be. And it isn't part of a giant plan.

It just is.

I still love God even though I don't understand this. And though we don't understand it now, I hope with all my heart, we can see the beauty of life again.

Love is beautiful. Love is precious. Love can be so, so, terribly sad. To have felt immensely hollow, completely sad, and yet SO overfilled with LOVE as Roark left this world is surprising. We felt his last breath, and it was filled with love. His love surrounded us and embraced us. It is the worst kind of homesickness and longing to feel his love again.

We would give anything to have him here. To have Roark healthy and in our arms. Panic overtakes me.

Our hearts ache with an undeniable amount of pain we wish no other person would ever, ever, ever have to feel. To hold your child as they leave this world and feel their lifeless body on your skin — it's suffering in the most underestimated, misunderstood way.

We had twenty-three days of everything, and felt every wrenching minute taken away from us in a flash. I have felt every spectrum of life in that short time. The most intense love the moment he was born. Immense pride as parents. Helpless pain in watching him suffer. Total grief in letting him go.

Though it's undeniably unfair and incomprehensible — the last six weeks of pain were worth every second to have felt any of Roark's love. To see Russ as a daddy. To have been a mommy. To have shared and witnessed our combined flesh. With him here, we felt every positive emotion love has to offer (except relief). Every second was worth it to have felt the greatest joy in life.

You know that Eric Clapton song, Tears In Heaven? It's on repeat in my ears. I wonder when it will leave. Part of me hopes right now. I need to stop feeling pain. The other part hopes never. I am afraid I will forget what he feels like, smells like, and looks like.

The only thing worse than this horrific situation is watching Russ suffer, too. Thank you for holding us up through all of this. Thank you for continuing to embrace us as we grieve.

And to our sweet, forever in our hearts, little lion man, Roark — thank you, baby boy, for all the gifts of love and strength you instilled in us. The world is a sad place to have lost you, but a better place to have had you.

All of our hearts, mommy & daddy;
D & R

That was the note I wrote to our closest friends and family the night Roark passed — and it just fell out of me. And I've reflected on the responses we received many, many times. It was July 2014 when I wrote it. And still, the words of our loved ones have uplifted me and held me when I have been crumbled and in tears. Our honesty created honesty. *Love begets love.*

"It is unfair, and I don't understand why."
"Your grace has inspired my journey."
"I am holding my children tighter."
"Your marriage inspires mine."
"Roark touched our lives."
"You've brought us along on a heart-wrenching and also beautiful journey. We are thankful."
"We will always remember Roark"
"We keep you and Russ in our prayers — hourly."
"We c a n n o t imagine."
"I am in awe and proud of you."
And . . . "I will ask my son to look out for Roark in Heaven."

Powerful connections created. Roark was impossibly tiny, and yet perfectly impactful. We still receive messages that he is a reminder to live presently, purposefully, and full of gratitude. Roark shined in only **twenty-three** days. He inspired and taught and shared so much love.

Perhaps it is because his passing was filled with love, and I wasn't expecting it. I guess I didn't know what to expect. I had never held someone as they transitioned. Our little lion was leaving us. When Roark's soul moved on, it was like a sigh of relief came out of him. Love surrounded us. It was everything warm and comforting in a moment that has felt too intimate to share. I have always said it was really big. *It was a really big moment.*

The lion characterization came early; when I was pregnant and we were suggesting baby names, my sister indulged the name Roark to symbolize "roar!" And when I was admitted with preeclampsia at twenty-three weeks(!) Russ wrote the mantra *Hakuna Matata* on my hospital board. He was determined to make it to viability and to have my health turn around. Hospitals are the most stressful places (especially when you're fighting for your own life and the life of your unborn child). Not exactly the place to help lower blood pressure. But no matter. Russ turned my hospital room into a spa. He massaged me day and night. He brought in my good friend and acupuncturist to help. My sister brought homemade muffins and freshly pressed juices. My parents drove two hours each day to stay with me. *Hakuna Matata; no worries.*

And then it happened. Roark needed to be born, or he would likely die in utero. Roark came via emergency c-section, a micro-preemie. And then he let out a surprising cry. A lion's roar.

Russ rushed to the Neonatal Intensive Care Unit (NICU) with him as my sister held my hand through another hour or longer of being closed up (I had bleeding that wouldn't clot due to a mistaken hepharine shot given by a nurse that morning). It would be an entire day before I held him. My chest constricted in pain seeing such a tiny baby. It also simultaneously bolstered in immediate pride. *Our boy.*

Without provocation, the nurses had drawn a lion on his isolette card. Our little lion was fighting so hard. And he did so, until he was suffering more than he was fighting. When he passed, I felt a *roar* of pain — and of supreme love. Our motto shifted from *Hakuna Matata* to *Roar Forever.*

MIRACLES

We left the hospital in total shock. It was a beautiful summer day; as we headed toward our home in the foothills, RVs and vans full of families passed us on the way to the mountains. I remember thinking, *these people have no idea.* The darkness of life I had never known now encompassed me. I remember thinking, *I will never be happy again.*

It was as bad as it gets.

I spent the following weeks in delusional pain. *Feeling the void;* every moment was spent wishing I could go back in time.

We distracted ourselves with anything and everything to not feel shattering pain.

Family and friends dropped by, and my sister called me daily to make sure I was still here.

I had a lot of guilt surrounding my body failing me, and us, and Roark. I whispered in the dark of the night for Roark to come back to me. That I was sorry. Russ knew this and reminded me relentlessly that it wasn't my fault. His forgiveness and acceptance helped me forgive myself.

His pain from losing his son — a boy holding so many dreams — was hard for me to help him with. Nature was his church. It became mine, too. I talked out loud to Roark. And soon Russ did, too. The ebbs and flow of our grief were like our union; we supported each other in waves as we could, in our own ways. Russ led me to accepting what was. I led him to the spiritual connectedness we now had with the other side. He is the only person in the world who knows exactly what my heart feels. And I for him. The intimacy is irreplaceable.

Those fresh weeks still bring me to tears. I mourn our son, and also the people we were before. Our naivety gone. Our ease. Our childlike wonderment and optimism. All of who we were transitioned, too. And looking back, this also brings me so much joy. We've come so far. We are stronger. We are wiser. We are more resilient. *We are layered.*

"The cracks are where the light gets in," Leonard Cohen sang. It is so true. I was cracked wide open in love. Grief is love you cannot quite grasp. And very slowly, without my even recognizing, the light came pouring back in.

A few weeks after Roark passed, a work mentor called me. He was crying, and he said, "There is a lot of devastation when you lose someone. I want you to know something, Danielle. There is *magic* in that madness. And there are also inspiring moments. And they become fleeting after a while. Don't lose that. Stay connected to that. Stay connected to how you feel right now. There is no comparison to this kind of clarity. When you lose someone so traumatically, life is clearer than ever before."

This shifted how I was feeling about Roark's passing. I opened up.

I opened up to healing.

I began writing everything I felt. Some of it was publicly posted. Most were just notes and letters to myself and Roark. It helped — and it still does. I became a student of grief. I wanted to know what other parents felt. I wanted to see the survivors before us. Luckily for me, I connected online with parents who were grieving in a similar way.

It also helped that little lions followed us everywhere. You may think that's just a coincidence. And I might've, too. Only they appeared when we needed them the most. In dark streets across the globe, in the arms of the child in front of us, in music during *cry rides*, and as symbols of the other boys gone too soon. I still acknowledge lions as Roark gently reminding us of his spiritual being. Miracles, if you keep your heart open to them. And luckily for me, I did.

GRIEF, GRATITUDE, GRACE

Later that fall, I found a lump on my neck. Or rather, *in*. My doctor examined it and immediately sent me for an ultrasound. The next day, I was referred to an otorhinolaryngologist (ENT) specialist to have the lump biopsied. In those fast-paced days of appointments, I wasn't scared. I was just angry. Also, not surprised. Life felt cruel and random.

I flew solo to Abu Dhabi the day after my biopsy. I was meeting Russ there. He was working, and we were travelling around Turkey afterward. I did not sleep at all on the flights. I was dwelling in my agony and also coming to peace with my demise. I was going to die. I would be joining Roark. He had fulfilled his journey, and I was about to fulfill mine.

I landed in Abu Dhabi to a voicemail from my doctor to call her back. It was mid-afternoon in U.A.E. and the middle of the night in Calgary. I waited. I sweated. My doctor connected the following day with good news: a benign mass that they could drain. *I wasn't dying.*

I cried. Because I realized I wasn't afraid to die anymore. Before Roark, death was the end; now it was a reunion. A connection to the other side that lifted all the fear. A piece of me healed in that moment. Fear dissipated. Love grew.

I have come to realize life *has many phases. And death is just one of them.*

Abu Dhabi shared its strikingly wealthy dichotomy with us. Lavish hotels, the most magnificent Grand Mosque, and also shanty towns of workers in conditions we couldn't imagine. Sometimes in life, perspective is handed to you so obviously, you take it obligingly. Touring ancient Christian and Islamic sites, I felt God returning to me in a form of understanding and love I hadn't felt before. Not in a religious context but rather via several vehicles.

One of the most profound moments happened just outside the Grand Bazaar. Amongst the trash on the street, I saw a young mom, her toddler girl, and her infant. The mom nursed the infant while begging for money. My own milk was still running, and I felt it flow in agony as we walked from her. I wanted so badly to take her baby and girl home with us. To a place of no begging, and of so much more.

I felt perspective flood me.

I had lost Roark. WE had lost Roark.

Yet we still had so much.

So many gifts of grace in our grief, through gratitude. *Grief, gratitude, grace. This was my path, more than I even knew at that time.*

One day not long after our trip, I woke up feeling hope. It surprised me and uplifted me. One good day lent itself to the promise of more good days.

I read once that you change for two reasons. Either you learn enough that you want to, or you've been hurt enough that you have to. Both now applied to me. I didn't want to be someone drowning in sadness, with everyone knowing my story just from looking at me. So I clung to every piece of evidence that showed I would be okay. Every earth angel who helped me feel hope became a beacon of light.

WHY ME

As the fall moved to winter; another shift. I went through a long period in which I said, *Why Me? Why Me? Why me, why me, why me?*

A friend of mine stopped me in my tracks.

And she said, "Why not you? Why not you to have such loss to see such joy in the world? Why not you to feel such suffering to know there is grief, and then growth?" And although I wasn't ready to hear this message, I thought about it a lot.

Now when I think about what would've been, or what could have been with Roark — because he would've been four years old now — it feels heavy and sad. Whereas when I think of him next to me *right now*, I think of him as a full, energizing spirit. A brave and super wise whole being. It makes me feel at peace, even joyful. We fully live by this now: *We honour his spirit, we don't create ghosts.*

Five days after Roark passed was my thirtieth birthday. When my sister gave me a birthday tribute, she labelled me **a warrior**. It empowered me. I didn't know it at the time, but it really did. One of the best things that others did for Russ and me was to tell us how proud they were of us, how they saw us as strong, what courage we had, how we inspired them to feel more gratitude. All of those things reinforced those thoughts in our heads that made us feel like warriors.

There are times I allow myself to be a victim. I lock myself away and ignore the outside world. I still do. Pity parties are my indulgence, and I am totally at ease with them. I also remind myself that I am a hero of the worst kind of tragedy. My life will never be mediocre. It has more mountains and valleys than I could have ever imagined. *I am a warrior.*

A friend shared the following analogy, and it's one of those perfectly held things I needed to hear.

At first, grief is like a huge boulder — unmanageable and too heavy to carry. It keeps you paralyzed and is exhausting. But it doesn't stay that way. It transforms *with* you, becoming lighter and easier to carry. Until one day, you realize it's much more like a marble in your pocket. Always with you, never gone. Though much lighter. This marble will be oh so shiny, absolutely adored, immensely loved, and always needed.

I love this analogy. I am transforming, and so is my grief. My grief isn't boulderous anymore. And although not yet light, it is completely shiny already.

Now when I am faced with trauma — I know I am resilient, and I know I will survive. Instead of feeling overwhelmed and angry — I now feel deeply empathetic and also fully aware (and accepting) of any outcome. Life is not perfect. And *that* is beautiful. Growth happens from trauma. Raw joy is felt after total devastation.

> *"Happiness can be found in the darkest of times, if one only remembers to turn on the light."* (Dumbledore, Harry Potter).

One year after Roark was born, we flew to Iceland to sit in the hot springs and adventure through its caves and on its ice fields. To toast our little lion man with a roar of courage. When we returned, my jet lag didn't lift.

I was pregnant.

If my life is a book, Roark is the title. And every chapter is different now.

~Dedicated to the earth angels and guiding angels who have pulled me from despair and shown me the power of love, hope, and allowing joy back in. When you're visiting Cochrane, Alberta, look for the picnic table high on the riverbank. Roark Russell Williams. May many families share love and joy here. Look to the stars, feel the river, smell the rain, play in the snow, And always, with courage and kindness:

ROAR FOREVER

Section 4
OUR IMPERFECT PASTS DO NOT DEFINE US

FEATURING

Jillian West

Charleyne Oulton

Sherri Marie Gaudet

Samantha Amaraegbu

Shayla Wey

Lisa Aamot

OPENING COMMENTARY BY

Sabrina Greer

We all have a past. Memories, experiences, moments, some fragmented, others vividly detailed — each of these pieces crucial to our psyche and responsible for shaping our very being. Some of these are beautiful, and others are, well, downright ugly. But these pieces, while they influence and set the foundation for who we are, need not define us. I often think of it as art. Some of the most sought-after and expensive art happened by accident. A rogue brush stroke, a crack in the marble, or a random smudge. *Perfect* only in the eyes of its admirers. It is okay to forever be a work in progress, to be constantly evolving, growing, and changing. It is okay to become slightly weathered and patinated over time; most art does become more valuable with age. The important thing to remember about art is that it is completely subjective. What is beautiful to one may be hideous to the next, and the only one who can attach any importance, any symbolism to signify its substance is the one gazing at it.

Our canvases may not be blank. They're primed by our experiences, our suffering, our challenges, and our growing pains. Having a textured canvas gives it some character; besides, it can always be painted over. We need to stop trying to be a Picasso or a Monet, stop trying to be what everyone else is, stop trying to fit into the mold society believes we should squeeze into, and for the love of all things beautiful, we need to stop comparing ourselves to everyone else. We need to own our imperfect past and all its pieces, in all its glory. We need to own our stories and our journeys and unapologetically share them with the world. Your story may be the Mona Lisa to someone else and by keeping it under a rug, you are doing a disservice.

The following six and final chapters express exactly this. These authors have all overcome the odds that were stacked against them. These brave mamas share their authentic journeys of their personal gradient from dark to light. The strokes on their canvases that charted the trajectory of their lives and brought them to where they are today. These stories will inspire you to move forward and paint a new picture. While we cannot change our past, we can embrace every piece of it as a lesson. We have the ability to change the future, to start over, and to love every layer of our beings. We have the internal power to paint over what no longer serves us, no longer aligns with us and our being, and to start fresh. You are unique and beautiful; you are a work of art, Mama!

16

SHADOW WORK

by Jillian West

"The skeletons in your closet can in fact become the soldiers in your army."

Jillian West

Jillian is a mother of three girls and a wife to James West. She has a background in early childhood education and social services. She is an active member of the recovery community in Vancouver, Canada and is passionate about helping women recover from alcoholism and drug addiction. She works part-time as a personal trainer specializing in postpartum fitness. She is an aspiring philanthropist and aims to start a nonprofit organization that helps women and men exit the sex trade; she is also realizing a long-time dream of becoming a published author with this project. You can keep up with Jillian on her successful blog, her social channel of choice, Instagram, and future writing endeavors within the *You've Got This, Mama* community.

www.soberliciousmama.com
ig: soberliciousmama
fb: Soberlicious Mamas Support Group

~ I would like to dedicate my chapter to my husband, James; you saved me from myself back then, and you continue to do so today. You're my everything, thank you for creating the Little's with me. To my father, Larry, I'm sorry I drank "at" you for all those years. I'm grateful for our mutual forgiveness and the relationship we have today; thank you for being such a great granddad to my girls. To my mum, for never turning your back on me. To my dear friend Alex B. for "chopping up" the magic blue book with me. To my twin, Karen, I'm so grateful we both made it out! To the most resilient warriors, my niece, Presley, and my firstborn, Shae. Lastly, to the incredible women in my life who walk beside me, you know who you are.

*"No matter how far down the scale we have gone we will
see how our experience can benefit others"*
~ the Promises, Page 84/85 of the big book of Alcoholics
Anonymous

E ver since I can remember, I felt different. Like I was never the right size;
no matter how hard I tried, I just never fit in. Even though I grew up
alongside my twin sister and appeared to have friends, I just always felt
alone. My dad was an Army dad, stoic and devoid of emotion for the most
part, excluding anger, which was an emotion he evoked that we were all
too familiar with. As a young girl, whenever I was around my dad, I felt like I
wasn't enough — not good enough, not smart enough, not pretty enough. I
felt like no matter what I did, I could never measure up.

We had a pretty normal childhood; my earliest memory is when we
moved out of the PMQs in Alberta to our rancher home in a cul-d-sac on
Swanson Street in Chilliwack, British Columbia, where my parents still live
today. We were six years old. We lived by a forest which is all developed now,
but back in the summer of 1983, it was our playground! I recall finding a copy
of Playboy magazine in the forest, and as I leafed through the pages in absolute curiosity and awe of these beautiful, perfect, naked women, that feeling
of not being good enough washed over me once again. I was ten years old.
At eleven, my sister and I had our first taste of liquor (a kiwi cooler, to be
precise, and on my parents' friends' boat no less); for the first time in eleven
years, I immediately felt a sense of comfort and confidence that I had never

known I always craved. That day on the boat was one of my fondest memories. The sun shone, laughter was the soundtrack of choice — my parents and their friends having a good time while my sister and I sipped the delicious kiwi cooler we were given to share with careless delight! Little did I know that liquor would become a luxury I could no longer afford because I would eventually develop a thirst so insatiable, I would do anything to quench it.

High school was a pretty tumultuous time for our family. My twin and I surrounded ourselves with people who drank like we did and got in trouble like we did; we would gravitate toward older friends with criminal records. Looking back, I think we chose to hang around these "going nowhere fast" types so we could in some way feel superior and less like the *losers* we were becoming. I recall sitting around after dinner one night when my mother yelled from the TV room, "Girls, wasn't that boy just over here yesterday?" It was our old friend, Norm. His face was plastered on the television on a Crime Stoppers alert. Ah, the lesser companions, how we loved them so. It made us look better in the eyes of our parents and made it easier for them to blame our bad behavior on the people we hung out with.

I wish I could have foreseen how my insatiable thirst, this beguiling disease, would take me lower than the belly of a snake. Eventually, it would become clear that we were, in fact, the lesser companions. My parents were frustrated and fed up with our behavior and were at their wits end. At the insistence of my dear old mum, my sister and I applied for colleges in Vancouver and by the end of the summer of 1997, we were packed up and shipped off to live life on life's terms in the big city. I remember making a pact with my sister that we would never drink or do drugs again, nor would we ever speak of our crazy past with anyone we met. We were determined to clean up our act. However, the disease of alcoholism is a cunning foe; it wasn't even a week before we found alcohol and drugs, our resolve to live a clean, sober life flushed down the drain, and addiction and impulse ran the show again.

It was in college that I met a girl who would forever change the course of my life as I knew it. She mentioned she had been making a significant amount of money giving topless massages at a place downtown. I was curious and more than willing to follow her after class one day to her workplace. I was hired immediately, and I walked out with fistfuls of hundred dollar bills on my very first day on the job. I would love to say that all I had to do was give topless massages, but that would be a lie. I told myself I would just work there until I finished college. Graduation came and went, but I never did quit this place. If, upon meeting that girl who essentially *turned me out*, I could foresee the future and know that one day of "happy endings" would turn into a lifetime of being soulless, entrenched in the sex trade, and wrapped up in that lifestyle, I would've spun around on my heels and run away from her as fast as I could.

I will spare you the details of the "work" I would do for almost two decades, but I will say this: What began as a somewhat glamorous, ego-stroking, independent, exciting way to earn a living quickly became a shameful, dangerous, and lonely existence with room only to feed my ever-increasing drug and alcohol habit and zero room for self-love or the possibility of turning my life around.

When things got really bad, I decided to move to England. You see, I still didn't realize I had a disease. I thought I had a problem and that problem was Vancouver, my environment. Swearing off drugs, alcohol, and the way I had been living, I said goodbye to Vancouver and moved to jolly old England, all determined to change and turn over a new leaf! It wasn't more than two weeks into my fresh start when I found myself back at the bottle and working in a brothel.

I obtained a work visa and was placed at a bed-and-breakfast type hotel called Gravetye Manor near East Grinstead. It was my intention to work behind the bar there, stay out of trouble, save money, and travel on my days off. It was my intention to turn my life around. I wanted so badly to have a *normal* life! I remember choosing England because I assumed there would be no language barrier — boy, was I wrong! The majority of the staff were Polish or French and spoke little to no English. I felt so lost, lonely, and out of place.

I recall beginning my shift behind the empty bar each morning. I had gone about four days without a drink, and this beautiful, expensive bottle of cognac called Louis Tres started calling my name from the top shelf of the bar. I began sneaking sips here and there during my shifts. The sips turned into gulps, until one morning when I entered the bar, I looked up and saw that someone had placed a little note in front of my beloved bottle: "Quit drinking me!" I didn't know whether to be embarrassed or angry, but all I did was crumple up the note and toss it in the trash. I smirked to myself thinking, *Well, at least the management is polite.*

Shortly after the incident, management informed me that they thought I must try my hand at being a chambermaid. They were on to me indeed. I felt a bit like *Alice in Wonderland* after this experience and my craving for more took over; I had spiraled down the rabbit hole. Liquor stopped being a luxury; it became a necessity, and I started drinking whatever I could get my hands on.

I met a Turkish man who was working at the bed-and-breakfast as a pastry chef; he spoke good English, as he had lived in Britain most of his life. We began a relationship and shortly after, we left our jobs at Gravetye and moved to Brighton. I found out that I was pregnant a couple weeks after we moved in together. I got a job at a nightclub where I met a beautiful Lithuanian woman who I swear sniffed me out. She invited me to come visit her after work because she had an opportunity for me. Enter the brothel. Bam! I was right back into the lifestyle I knew all too well, but this time, I was with child.

I flew back home after I saved enough cash to do so and moved in with my parents. I swore to myself yet again that this would be the last time; I was determined to change my ways. I had to. I *wanted* to. Being pregnant was the best feeling ever. I hadn't felt so alive, so great in probably a decade. No more hangovers from hell, no more selling my body, no more substance abuse. For the first time in my entire life, I felt like I had meaning and purpose.

My beautiful baby girl, Shae, was born on November 23, 2006. She was my world. I was so in love with her and I wanted to be the best mother to her! After about three months of living with my parents, I moved back to Vancouver with big plans to use my schooling and run a little home daycare to support us. I wish I knew then what I know now. The following information is my understanding of alcoholism from the big book of Alcoholics Anonymous:

"That I have a disease that starts with the phenomenon of craving, and the mental obsession and that once I put a drink or a drug in my body I cannot stop, that I also suffer from a spiritual malady, a soul sickness and unless I find a power greater than myself I am doomed."

You see, for us alcoholics, to drink is to die. To make a long story short, the home daycare never happened and I went back to being an escort at a high-end parlour called Madame Cleo's. I became completely entrenched in the lifestyle; my only saving grace was that my beautiful baby girl was in full-time childcare so I was only responsible for dropping her off and picking her up from daycare. I remember the countless nights I spent weeping by her crib as I watched her sleep, crying out, "Why can't you be enough for me to stop?!" I would always be filled with such guilt and remorse the next day, when I would swear off drinking. A couple days would pass, and I would forget the pain and chaos of it all and be back at the bottle again.

It was 2011, and my twin sister and I had been living a life of unimaginable darkness and desperately needed help! We researched places that could help us with drug addiction and drinking; a list of Alcoholics Anonymous (AA) and Narcotics Anonymous (NA) meeting centres came up, and we chose one close to our house. Filled with just the right amount of desperation, we walked up the steps of The Vancouver Recovery Club and into our first recovery meeting. It was here that I first learned about "the disease of addiction" and also met others who suffered from this disease, just like me. Some were actually multiple years clean and sober! This not only amazed me, it filled me with hope! I felt relieved to know I was not some horrible, crazy person and thanked God I wasn't alone.

I believe my sister and I went about two weeks clean and sober before picking up the dreaded devil again. You see, no matter how much we loved our little girls, the disease was more powerful than our love for them. At least at the time, I felt like no human power could save me, that I was beyond human aid. I spent the next couple years running on complete self-will.

Two years later, in 2013, I met the man who would become my husband. Our paths crossing, I believe wholeheartedly, was meant to be and was my higher power, the Universe, God, whatever you want to call it at work. I fell for him almost instantly; I even introduced him to my daughter, Shae. I tried to hide my issues at first, but after the first few times we drank together, he identified that I had a problem: I didn't drink like other people and was an addict.

He stuck around despite my wild and uncontrollable ways. We would have some good days in between my self- destruction and self- sabotage. He would tell you today that it was the glimpses of *that* woman he saw during those few and far-in-between "good days" that he fell in love with. The one who was kind and giving — a good mom and a nice person to be around. It was *those* glimpses that kept him around, and I am grateful he was able to see past all the masks and drama I constantly created. My disease wanted him gone, and when I was in my active addiction, I was horrible. I became this Tasmanian Devil, spinning around destroying everything and everyone in my way. Then when I would "calm down," I would look around and wonder why everything and everyone around me was broken or wanted nothing to do with me.

After some months of this craziness, James threatened to leave. He was the first person to ever stand up to me, and his words scared me. "If you don't go back to recovery and get the help you need, you are going to lose your daughter, and I am not going to be part of the madness."

I knew in my heart he was right, and so I went back to the rooms of AA. I went to meetings, and I basically white-knuckled it. Shortly after, I became pregnant with my second daughter. Jaida Rose was born on January 27, 2015; we were so in love with her and with each other. But I suffered a bit of the baby blues and I started isolating myself, not going to meetings, not reaching out. She was about two months old when I relapsed; it was the most brutal bender yet. I cannot even tell you what went on over the next few months because I was out of my mind. I was out of control, like fire destroying everything in its wake. James was scared; my disease was more powerful than his love for me or my love for him and the girls. I had broken Shae's heart yet again, and I could barely stand myself. My remorse and shame were so great, they swallowed me whole. I didn't want to face my family and I couldn't live with myself anymore.

Insanity and still more depravity were followed by a suicide attempt when my second daughter was approaching her first birthday. I saw that history was about to repeat itself. I had really hit my rock bottom this time, and I wanted out. James held my hand January 19, 2016, and I managed to get through the day without a drink. I was putting my children to bed when there was a knock at the door; it was Car #86, and a police officer and a social worker were there to apprehend my children. By the grace of God, I was sober and invited them in, and we came up with a plan.

After they left, I literally fell to my knees and asked God for help. I promised I would do whatever it took to stay sober. I cried uncontrollably and felt defeated. The threat of losing my children gave me the gift of desperation I needed to begin changing everything. I have not sold myself since nor have I had a drink or a drug. Instead, I found myself an incredible sponsor who took me through the twelve steps and showed me a new way to live. I have women who have gone before me to teach me how to show up in my life today. I have sponsees whom I have had the privilege of taking through the twelve steps and who walk with me on this road to recovery. I have had to get some outside help and learn coping mechanisms and tools for dealing with life and making peace and amends with my past. I have had to learn valuable life skills such as forgiveness and self-acceptance. Most importantly, I had to learn to stop running the show. I have a higher power in my life whom I choose to call God. He is the director of my life today and for that, I am truly grateful.

I spent the majority of my life letting everyone use me but God; now I pray for His will for me and the grace and strength to carry that out. I have purpose and direction in my life today, and my children have the mother they have always deserved.

My third daughter was born in September 2016, and James and I were married in 2017. I am honestly living a life I never thought could be mine! When I first came into recovery, I came to take; now I stay to give. For me, helping others has become a way of life! The gifts of sobriety are bountiful, and I find the beauty in everything today, both positive or negative. For example, the fact that my children don't have to ask me whether they can have a sip of something on the counter or the fact that when I go somewhere, they know that I am going to return to them in the exact same state in which I left are two of the most beautiful and reassuring things ever. I never thought I'd ever arrive at this place.

My eldest daughter has her mama back, and she is trusting me again. She is so resilient and beautiful, and I am so grateful for her forgiveness and the relationship we have today! I cannot say I'm sorry anymore; however, I can make amends to her and my husband by staying sober, one day at a time.

My relationship with my parents has also changed immensely, and I thank them for never turning their back on me! They even came to my two-year sobriety cake celebration and for the first time in my life, my father told me he is proud of me! These priceless gifts are what my sobriety gives me today. Today I am a part of, today I have a sense of belonging, today I am right-sized, and today, for the first time in my life, I feel like I DO matter and I AM worthy. Today, I help other mothers in various ways — whether it's connecting through social media, which I use as a platform for sobriety, or through the online support group I created for mothers in recovery. I have service positions in the fellowship of AA and I speak on panels at hospitals and detox centers, sharing my experience, strength, and hope with those still suffering. I also have the privilege of going to schools and speaking to at-risk youth about the dangers of drugs and alcohol and the lifestyles that can come with addiction.

The freedom and strength I have found in sharing my story is immeasurable. Owning my truth has helped me shed the heavy armor of remorse, shame, and guilt that so many of us, as women and especially as mothers, get weighed down by. The only things that matter now are what I can do to help others recover from alcoholism, how I can share my experience to show women it is possible to exit the sex trade, how I can provide hope to mothers when they want to give up, and most importantly, how my family feels about me and how the God of my understanding sees me. *This* is where I get my worth and validation from today, not the bottle or drugs.

A very dear friend reminded me recently that no one can tell your story except you. This is my story to tell. I am living proof that the skeletons in your closet can in fact become the soldiers in your army and that indeed, you've got this, Mama!

17

BEGINNING AGAIN

by Charleyne Oulton

"Learn to trust your intuition; it is possible to love someone and leave them."

Charleyne Oulton

Charleyne Oulton, "Coach Charley Brown", is a confident, happy, and divorced mom of three children who lives on beautiful Vancouver Island, BC. She is genuine, experienced, and passionate about creating and maintaining a life full of peace and joy. She is also an appreciated health and wellness coach with *It Works Global*. She is a multi-time co-author with Golden Brick Road Publishing House and has been published in *On Her Plate* and *Her Art of Surrender*. She is also writing in upcoming books to be published in 2019. Charleyne is a regular contributor for YGTMAMA blog. A well-known photographer and a Reservist in the Royal Canadian Navy, Charleyne wears many hats. Even through the busy and beautiful chaos of raising a family and adjusting to life after divorce, she loves life and is passionate about encouraging others to thrive.

www.coachcharleybrown.com
ig: @coach.charley.brown | #coachcharleybrown
fb: coachcharleybrown
Portraiture by Katie Jean Photography, Mill Bay BC

*"The Bhagavad Gita — that ancient Indian Yogic text —
says that it is better to live your own destiny imperfectly
than to live an imitation of somebody else's life
with perfection."*
~ Elizabeth Gilbert: Eat Pray Love

I remember the day my mom and dad sat my older brothers and me down to tell us they were getting a divorce. Even though I was just a young girl, six years old, I can remember parts of this conversation like it was yesterday. I can remember feeling itchy from the coarse fabric of our 1980s couch touching my arm. The tears rolling down my mother's face. The heart-breaking look in my father's eyes and giving him the longest hug before he walked out our front door. One of my brothers slammed his bedroom door, and the other was very silent. The horrible feeling that *this must somehow be MY fault.* I also remember blaming my now step-mom for the end of my parents' marriage.

I could not have been more wrong. She was *not* the reason my parents parted. However, I was just a child then and that was *my* truth. I think this position is common when children are dealing with divorce. Sometimes they blame themselves. Sometimes they blame one of the parents or their new partners. It's simply a coping mechanism. The end of my parents' marriage was the best thing that could have ever happened to them, but it would have been impossible to convince me of this at the time.

Now, as an adult, I understand this notion much better. In some situations, divorce is a selfish choice that hurts a family and breaks it apart, but sometimes, it is a choice that is much needed and helps improve everyone's life, health, and wellbeing.

What is right for *you?*

This is when you must listen to your gut and really examine your relationship and be honest with yourself. Is your current relationship building you up? Is it free of belittling, even in the heat of a disagreement? Is your partner gentle and patient with you, always? Do they celebrate who you truly are in spite of your idiosyncrasies? *Learn to trust your intuition.* It is possible to love someone *and* leave them. If you know you need to leave your marriage, or that it is ending, try looking at this choice as a positive start to a new and fulfilling life for you and your family rather than as a failure or act of sin.

Sometimes love nourishes your soul and flows freely. Sometimes love hurts and holds you back. Sometimes love is not enough. Once you realize you deserve better, letting go, walking away, and moving on will be the best decision ever, even if it feels terrifying. Be brave enough to start over and to create the life that you always dreamed of.

After all, you can live happily ever after, separately.

Family is family. Family is not determined by marriage, by paperwork, or even by blood. Family is not defined by the people with whom you share DNA. Rather, it is the people in your life who choose to be there. The ones who truly accept you for who you are, regardless of your mistakes or idiosyncrasies. The ones who would do anything to see you smile and who love you no matter what. I am fortunate enough to have a huge and loving family which includes two mothers and one father. All my parents love me. They have provided for me. They chose me when I was a young child, a rebellious teenager, a teen mother, and now an adult recovering from divorce. I am very lucky.

Parenting is one of the toughest jobs on the planet, requiring endless sacrifice and dedication. To raise successful and strong children, you need to devote countless hours and years to loving, supporting, and teaching them.

My second mom *chose* to love me. She chose my brothers, too. What an amazing woman to choose to devote herself to children whom she did not bear. The words "thank you" are not enough to express my deep gratitude. Nor are the words "I'm sorry" enough to make up for all of the anger and hurtful treatment in the beginning of our relationship.

Our relationship grew stronger year by year because my second mom did not give up on me or my siblings. She became another constant source of love in our world.

As *Dr Seuss said, "Unless someone like you cares a whole awful lot, nothing is going to get better. It's not."*

Surviving Divorce

I never wished divorce for my own children. I still do not wish this chaotic life for them. Yet it is our current reality. They, too, are *surviving* divorce and all that comes with it. I can honestly say that they are handling the chaos with more grace than I did at their age. Maybe it helps that I can truly empathize with them. I try to acknowledge their feelings daily. To listen to them and pay attention to *what* they say and *how* they say it. I have learned to appreciate each and every hug, kiss, drawing, picked flower, or handwritten note. For these are gifts straight from their hearts.

I also try to set a good example daily, whether that is focusing on my children, my own health and mental wellness, or how I talk about their biological father. I make sure the words I use about him are not hurtful or harmful for them to hear. I realize my children love him and are just as much a part of him as they are a part of me; although our marriage has ended, he is still a part of their world.

Dating After Divorce

Dating after divorce is a brand new experience. It is hard. Scary. Awkward. Fun. Exciting. A true mixture of emotions. Dating after divorce is often very hard for children, too. *When is it okay to introduce a new partner to your children?* This is the million-dollar question, as they say. In my opinion, there is no *right* answer. My advice is to not rush the process. Allow yourself and your new relationship time to grow. What is right for me and my family might not be what is right for you and for your family. In fact, with every child, family, and situation, it is a different answer.

My children were introduced to my ex-husband's first partner (post-divorce) way too fast (in my opinion). I did not get to be a part of that decision or introduction, and I had to comfort very confused and emotional children when they returned home. I felt such anger and resentment. I remember thinking, *How dare another woman parent my children and pretend to be their mother and pretend to live my life?* I struggled with this, a lot. Yet as time went on, I realized that there is no stronger bond than the bond between a mother and a child. So I decided to stop second-guessing myself. The only things I could control were my reactions and my relationship with my children. I learned from this experience that my children needed to be included in any new relationships that I might have and talked to about it in advance. In this chapter of life, my children had lots of questions and needed lots of reassurance. They felt much resentment towards my ex-husband's partner. They blamed her for the end of our marriage, much like I did as a young girl.

Isn't It Funny How Your Life Can Come Full Circle?

I poured myself into my children, who were only nine, ten, and twelve years old at the time. Their life was changing drastically in all areas, and I just wanted them to know that some things would never change. I became their constant in a world that now seemed to be spinning out of control. I focused on my relationship with my children, ensuring that we always had and have open communication. We started counselling. I took numerous parenting courses for families who are transitioning and read countless books and blogs on parenting through divorce. I think it is important to surround yourself with others who are going through the same thing. I reached out to my local health unit, who had recommendations for programs my children and I might benefit from.

People will walk in and out of your life, but those who matter will stay." ~ Charleyne Oulton

A Package Deal

When I started dating and met the man I hope to spend my future life with, I was *terrified* to introduce him to my children. Thoughts and anxieties spiraled through my head.

What if our relationship does not last, and my children get hurt? What if his family cannot accept me and my divorce? What if my children do not respect him? How will he fit into my chaotic and now broken world?

I talked to my family and support network a lot about this. It took a long time for me to begin healing from my divorce and put my broken heart back together. I had trust issues and felt anxious to start over. I journaled, prayed, and talked to my kids about dating. I also talked to my new boyfriend a lot and chose to be very honest with him right from hour one. *My children are my all, and he needed to respect that I was "a package deal."* I came with three kids, baggage, an ex-husband, and a whole lot of drama.

He reassured me that he would take it slow with my kids, that he felt honoured to meet them and was ready to meet them. We talked about our short-term and long-term goals and found that we had a lot in common. I talked to my ex-husband about this as well, and I decided to introduce our children during a family dinner so they would have lots of support from extended family during this introduction. It was a more casual meeting this way. Nobody felt any pressure (except my boyfriend, I'm sure).

What a brave man he was, to come over for Christmas dinner on Christmas Day to a house full of extended family. In one swoop, he meet my mother, her boyfriend, my brother and his wife, my children, my aunts on my mother's side, and one of my cousins. Just in case that was not enough of an overwhelming welcome for him, I also had some of my best friends over. Welcome to the family, literally.

His Choice

I will never have the words to capture what I thought and what I felt when I held my children for the first time. Nor will I ever be able to describe what joy I feel in my heart when I watch my children and now spouse together. The bond they have is beautiful. He *chooses* them daily, and they are beginning to grow a deep and genuine love for him. It has not always been easy. Not for him. Not for our children. Not for myself. We have our struggles, and it is still an adjustment even though we have been together for twenty-three months. Choosing to become a parent to someone else's children is a big decision. I am not a stepmother, but I do love a man who has chosen to love my children as his own. He joined our chaos without hesitation, and as an outsider. My children were nine, ten, and twelve years old when he met them, ages that are known to be quite impressionable. My children and I have many years of memories and experiences of which he is simply not a part. We encourage the children to talk about these memories freely and to acknowledge that there were some great times before he joined our family. We have had to reassure our children on numerous occasions that he is *not* trying to replace their biological father and that their dad is always their dad, no matter what; my now spouse is here to join our family and love them as well.

I am so thankful for his love and support. He is a good role model, provider, and friend to my children. The bond he has with each of my children is unique. One child calls him "Dadda" occasionally, the other child calls him by his name, and the third goes back and forth between his first name and "Dad." We have put zero pressure on the children. It's their choice. What will be, will be. We have house rules we enforce and all obey. I choose to allow him to co-parent with me. My children respond well to this. I think they are thriving and responding so well to the consistent love and care they receive in their lives from their whole support network.

That's the thing about co-parenting, and parenting after divorce. The structure and discipline, routine, and love needs to stay constant; otherwise we as adults, co-parents, and stepparents have to be very flexible. As the children grow into teenagers, who knows what they might choose, where they might reside, or what issues we might encounter. But I know in my heart that my children will continue to be successful because they are surrounded by people who love and respect them.

The D Word

I never liked the D word (divorce); it always seemed like an ugly word to me. And here I am, a thirty-two-year-old woman with this title. It's not what I would have chosen for myself, but ironically it was the best thing that ever happened to me. This massive life change forced me to put on my big girl panties and become independent for the first time as an adult. I was a teen mom and was with the same man since I was sixteen years old. I never had the chance to be alone or truly discover who I was as a woman outside of being someone's wife or a mother.

Change is hard; it challenged me and terrified me immensely. *Who am I? How do I want our normal day-to-day life to unfold? What do I want to do with my life? Where will I live? How will I provide for my family? What will my friends and family think?* I learned that I needed to become comfortable with being uncomfortable. Divorce is an uncomfortable process. Change can feel terrifying. Being courageous for yourself is not always the easy choice. Doing what is right for you sometimes can feel impossible and unattainable. But your ultimate happiness is worth fighting for, and so is your joy. Joy is *hope*. Joy is always within you.

Today is a good day to start walking away from anyone or anything that causes you more angst than joy.

So, dear, take a leap of faith, have patience, and get out there! Get to know yourself and other people. Be boldly vivacious. Live freely and fiercely. Try new things — you are not who you once were in or before your last relationship. You have evolved, your intentions and dreams have expanded even if you haven't fully realized them. Your soul has grown and is waiting to be heard, to be loved, to be seen, to gift you all the possibilities and talents that lie within you to live your best life. Raise your standards and re-evaluate what you are looking for. Take your time, have casual dates with different types of people. Relax, let loose, have fun, and keep it light. It could take time to learn how to communicate, flirt, and get to know someone again. Be honest with yourself and with them. I love meeting new people, but I can admit that I am cautious and tend to be reserved in the beginning of a friendship. I have learned to embrace and enjoy those little butterflies, and I am sure to acknowledge and recognize any emotions that arise. You will learn a lot about yourself as you start to date after a breakup. My only advice is to date someone who makes you feel confident, happy, and truly enjoys your company. Try not to compete or compare, but rather learn to embrace the current moment. Life is a gift, and being able to share it with another person is a true blessing.

Much Love,
Charleyne Oulton

~The encouraging and dedicated editors, publisher, designers, and lead authors at Golden Brick Road Publishing House richly deserve my praise and gratitude for yet another job well done. I sincerely thank all of you for your continued guidance and support. To my children, family, and friends: I am deeply thankful for you all; your unwavering love is never doubted. My love for you is endless.

18

LIFE HAPPENS

by *Sherri Marie Gaudet*

"*Life sometimes throws you curveballs, making tough decisions you couldn't make yourself.*"

Sherri Marie Gaudet

Sherri Marie believes you should always live in the present moment. She is positive to a fault and will always find a way to make even the most boring task fun. She is all about finding the good in even the worst of situations. Sherri Marie loves being around her friends, both new and old. She is outgoing and friendly and has no problem chatting with strangers. Sherri Marie is a 2x best-selling author, contributing to *I'm 30, Now What* and the original *You've Got This, Mama*. She has always been someone who sets her mind on something and will find a way to accomplish it, no matter how hard it is.

Although she didn't always know what she wanted to do when she *grew up*, Sherri Marie knew that she wanted to help people. She was always a risk-taker, often doing before thinking, believing nothing in the world was impossible, doing her best work when the odds were stacked against her. Sherri Marie tried out various career paths during her twenties before finally realizing that her talents were best spent helping others as an entrepreneur and business leader.

Sherri Marie is a national market developer/recruiter. She strives to help people believe in themselves and design lives they love.

www.lifestyleofsherrimarie.com
ig: @Lifestyleofsherrimarie
fb: SherriMarie

"Each day of our lives, we make deposits in the
memory banks of our children."
~ Charles R. Swindoll

They always say the things we want most in life are also the things we tend to push away. That you can't help what your heart feels, that love is unconditional and something you cannot always put into words. I always told everyone, "I don't want more kids, one and done." That was my motto. It started when my son was young and I found myself a single mom. Deep down, however, I always longed for more children, but it was easier to tell people they weren't for me. I figured if I could convince the world I didn't want more children, I could eventually convince myself, too.

Life has a funny way of working out. Sometimes the things that are meant to be in your life come about in ways you never imagined. My life over the last few years did not play out the way I imagined it would; yet in many ways, I'm certain it unfolded exactly how it was supposed to. If you told me a year ago that my once perfectly kept house would suddenly be a lived-in home full of love, I would have rolled my eyes at you. If you said that I would go from being barely present with one child to suddenly having three living with me, I would have laughed so hard that tears would have streamed down my face. If you had dared to say I would love two children to whom I didn't give birth as much as I love my own son, I would have told you that you were batshit crazy.

June 23, 2013 and July 19, 2013 are two days of my life I will never forget. On June 23, 2013, I held a welcome home party for my friend; that party
changed my life forever. On July 19, 2013, it was my son's sixth birthday; it
was also the day I found out I was pregnant. I had been in complete denial
for weeks; even that day, I was in denial. Looking back now, if I had the slight-
est idea I was pregnant, I would have waited until after my son's birthday to
find out. I most certainly would not have wanted to find out in his father's
bathroom while dropping him off to celebrate for the night.

Shock, disbelief, and complete panic are understatements to describe
my emotions at the time. I froze, the world stopped, and suddenly everything
around me went black. I sat on that bathroom floor sweating and shaking for
a few minutes, wondering how this could be happening. Only in the movies
do you get pregnant from having sex with someone one night, right? Wrong.

It was just a welcome home party for my good friend; we weren't supposed to cross the line with each other that night, and crossing the line was
not supposed to change our lives forever. The night I found out I was pregnant, I was supposed to go to a surprise birthday party for one of my friends.
I knew I could never go and pull off not doing shots all night without raising
suspicions — I was always the one egging everyone on at parties to do shots.
I called the dad of my unborn child and tried to convince him to blow off
the party and come over; he told me he was already blowing it off to hang
out with another girl. I couldn't be upset; we were not together, and I knew
they had been seeing each other. I tried to get the words to come out of my
mouth that we needed to talk, but they just wouldn't come. Instead I put
myself to sleep — let's be real, I sobbed myself to sleep that night, hoping
when I woke up, it would all be just a bad dream.

I woke up the next day and it was still my reality. I knew I couldn't just
ignore it, but I also knew I wasn't ready for another child. *Was I?* The next
few days of my life were a complete whirlwind; I felt every emotion under the
sun. One minute I was fine, excited even, and the next minute I found myself
sobbing and wondering why this was happening. I couldn't bring myself to
tell my friend (baby daddy) over the phone or through text message. And
my buddy, whom I had always spent so much time having fun with, suddenly
wasn't around every time I tried to hang.

Life sometimes tosses you curve balls, making tough decisions for you, decisions you can't make yourself or don't have the courage to make yourself. That is exactly what happened in this case. I lost my child, something I never expected to experience in my life. The emotions I felt were indescribable. I won't lie, for a few minutes I felt relief, but that was short-lived. Once that relief wore off, I felt a never-ending emptiness. I felt lonely, cheated out of an opportunity. I felt hollow.

I couldn't understand the emotions I was feeling. *How could I be so deeply attached to a child who was completely unplanned, even unwanted? How could I be so deeply attached to a child I hadn't ever met? How could my heart feel so completely empty?* I couldn't handle any of the emotions I was feeling and was afraid to confront what they meant, so I turned to partying; I needed an escape from reality. I even pushed my son away because being around him opened up a Pandora's Box worth of emotions. I felt so guilty for being "depressed" over my loss, which only led to more partying.

Eventually, I got through my crazy party stage and met someone with whom I settled down; however, kids were still not my jam, especially ones who would be around the same age my second child would have been. It might sound completely crazy to most, but in my heart, I knew my child who was too special for earth would have been a little girl.

I settled down with a firefighter — what a whirlwind of a relationship that was. I actually wrote all about it in my first book, *I'm Thirty, Now What.* My now-ex was best friends with his partner at work, whose girlfriend I was told, shortly into our relationship, was the yin to my yang and whom we had to meet because we would hit it off. The fire department wasn't just a job, it was a complete lifestyle. A lifestyle that many of my friends just didn't understand, so I was excited to make a new friend who "lived my life."

I'll never forget the day Lau messaged me; we instantly hit it off and said we had to make plans to meet soon. I was so excited about our conversation. I knew that we would get along well and our sons would hit it off, too. My son is an only child and bright beyond his years; I attribute this to how independent I had made him after my loss. It wasn't every day I met a child his age he would get along with. However, Lau's son had a similar personality, and it seemed like they would be a great match. There was just one huge issue for me — she had just recently had a baby girl. The irony that Lau's daughter was born a year to the date my child would have been born was emotionally overwhelming for me.

To this day, I have no idea what gave me the strength to visit them when they invited us over one Saturday afternoon. All I do know is that in my gut, it just felt right, and I have always been one to follow my instinct. I felt so many emotions that day; of course, the plan was to stay for an hour at most, and I had no intention of interacting with the new baby. Life, though, it never goes according to plan.

We walked in that day and before I knew it, I was on the floor playing with this beautiful baby girl. For the first time since losing my child, I was interacting with another baby, and it didn't feel like complete torture. We stayed a lot longer than an hour that day. It was the beginning of an incredible friendship between all of us, an incredible bond between me and my *mini bestie*, as I call her. The instant connection and bond we had, I can't put into words and never expected. It might sound like insanity to some, but I believe in my heart that this amazing little lady was brought into my life by my unborn child, my angel in heaven. Not to ever replace her, but to help me find peace with having a baby who was just too special for this earth.

I was lucky enough to be able to spend many days and even nights with her during the first two years of her life. As I mentioned earlier, firefighting is a lifestyle, not a job. Every day and night I spent with her, she helped me become a little more myself — who I once was before losing my child. I was lucky enough to witness her biggest milestones. The first time she spoke, the night she took her first steps, I even had the honor of snipping her hair for the first time. From the day we met, her mom let me play such an incredible role in her life, a role I can't put into words how much I value. We all know that children are sponges, soaking up so many things from the people they are around the most. I spent so much time with my mini bestie that she couldn't help but pick up some habits; saying "toodle loo" and chucking up the peace sign will forever be one of my favorite influences I have had on her.

I had been given a chance to be a huge influence on a child whom in my heart I knew had a connection with the baby I had lost. It was a connection that was brought into my life to give me peace. Then this past

November, I was lucky enough to have both her and her brother move in with us. For years, my son had begged me for a sibling; it broke my heart every time and I pushed him away because I couldn't handle the pain of my loss and he was too young for me to share it with him. Although these three children were obviously not siblings by blood, they were about to become siblings through experience.

I was in Florida for Thanksgiving when my best friend called and said she had ended her relationship and had no idea where they were going to go. Without hesitation, I said, "You guys are moving into my house." I returned from Florida a few days later to find that every aspect of life was different. My best friend had stayed home for the last three years and was suddenly tossed back into the workforce. She was lucky enough to land a job with decent pay. However, it meant that she was gone before the kids woke up and got home after they went to bed. This meant that ninety-eight percent of the time, it was just me and three children.

My life went from non-stop leisure and fun (remember, my son was very independent compared to most children) to pure, organized chaos. I went from having too much free time on my hands to not having a second alone. It was crazy, chaotic, and a complete one-eighty that happened in the blink of an eye. My life went from looking fabulous on the outside but feeling so empty inside to looking chaotic on the outside but feeling so full of love. My once perfectly clean and picture-perfect house was now messy and crazy. For the first time, my house felt like a home — a real home full of pure joy, love, laughter, and all the crazy chaos that comes with having three children under your care. I am not going to say every day is easy or runs smoothly, because that is not the case. No, most days I am running on empty physically, always in go-go-go mode with not a second to myself and by the time I finally end my day, I am beyond exhausted. Ironically though, I have never felt more alive.

It's funny how in life, we do things for people with the purest of intentions to help them, not thinking they would really be the ones helping you grow into the best version of yourself. Before I had three incredible humans call my house their home, I was selfish and self-centered in many ways. I didn't ever intend to be that way, but it was how life was. My son was independent and always ready to go wherever I sent him. To him, that was normal life and he didn't know anything different. I am mom enough to admit that there was a time I wasn't "Mom of the Year." I was so disconnected from mom life for a while that I could, in fact, go days without seeing him and be okay. I was so bitter about my loss that I put my needs and wants before being a mom. However, when my best friend and her kids moved in, there was no time for being selfish.

In the past nine months, I believe I have learned what life is truly about. Ironically, it is *not* any of the things I once thought. A perfect house doesn't matter; a home does. The laughter, the tears, the memories you make every day in a lived-in home last with you for a lifetime; a catalog-perfect house does not. There is no greater joy than watching kids have fun, not even realizing they are creating memories to last a lifetime; to them they are just having fun on a Monday night. Yes, of course, it's awesome to clean your house once and have it stay spotless, but where are the memories in that? Cleaning it one thousand times or spending hours troubleshooting why you have ants, only to find out that the boys hid candy wrappers in their rooms, is a memory you will laugh about for years.

Do I miss my crazy nights out on the town? Ironically, no. I am so much happier being home on Friday night playing a board game with the kids. I have a newfound respect for the television show *Are You Smarter Than A Fifth Grader?* Let me tell you, homework for a nine- and eleven-year-old is no joke. I got off easy before this year.

Is there something to be said about having perfectly folded bath towels and getting all your laundry done in two hours a week? Yes, of course. Call me crazy if you want, but if given the choice, I will choose the endless loads of laundry and less than perfectly folded towels because they were folded with the most love.

Has learning how to cook resulted in some dinner horror stories and the smoke detectors forever cheering me on? You betcha! But when we look back on the dinner disasters and laugh so hard our sides hurt, I would pick cooking every time.

Being able to go to the gym whenever you want is nice, but racing around after little humans is even nicer.

I recently met a really incredible guy who is everything I could have ever asked for and more, for the first time in a long time. As much as I liked him and knew he was what I was looking for, I wouldn't allow him to enter my life unless he understood the importance of my unique family. For the first time in many years, I wasn't selfish or self-centered; I knew at that moment I had come to peace with my loss. I knew for the first time since my loss that I was back to loving not just my son wholeheartedly but now these two other children as well.

The bond I share with all three children in my life is different, and I have learned that's okay. It doesn't mean I love one more or one less; the bonds we share are just different. It's just like life — no two friendships are the same.

The connection I have with my mini best friend is incredible and so real. I have never been religious; it's just never been my jam. And while religion still isn't my jam, she has taught me to believe in something greater than myself. Not a day goes by where I don't find myself spending a few minutes reflecting on how I truly believe my mini bestie was brought into my life by my child who was too special for earth. I know that she isn't my child; I know that she can never take that place, nor would I ever want her to. One thing I am one hundred percent certain of is this: she has helped my heart be full again, and I can only hope that the bond we share will stay as strong throughout her life as it is now. I can only hope to always be a positive influence on her life, no matter where life takes her. If I can help her make even just one less mistake in her life than I have, I will forever be at peace with my past and how life played out. She is much too young now to even realize what she has done for me, so my only hope is that one day when she is older, she knows that no matter what, I will always be there for her any way I possibly can.

The greatest lesson she has taught me is that love is love. Love is all-seeing, all-knowing, and pure. Love doesn't care if you are related by blood; it isn't something that can be forced. No, love is something that you feel, something that just happens. So, Mama, cherish those little ones, love them hard. Even when you feel you may not have another ounce of energy, of "you" left to give, trust me — you've got this! Lean into your children, let them be your anchor, and stay open to love, no matter the forms in which it comes into your life!

~ To my mini bestie . . . could never imagine life without you in it . . . I am thankful for the bond we share and all the memories we have made together.

19

BABIES SHOULDN'T HAVE BABIES

by *Samantha* Amaraegbu

"Don't ever let anyone tell you that you cannot make it, not even yourself."

Samantha Amaraegbu

Samantha Amaraegbu is a paralegal and aspiring author who currently lives in Québec, Canada. While finding her way through school, work, and being a mom, she never gave up on her dreams. Samantha works in the legal field but is always exploring new and challenging growth opportunities in different fields. With a variety of projects up her sleeve, Samantha will see them to fruition no matter what. Inspired and motivated by her child, Samantha is a mama who is driven, unstoppable, and relentless in pursuit of her dreams.

www.maisonduru.life | www.theglowup.ca
ig: x0xsamx0x

*" I didn't plan on being a single mom, but you have to
deal with the cards you are dealt the best way you can."*
~ Tichina Arnold

1:00 am:

Me: "Babe, I think something is wrong . . ."

Him: "What's wrong?"

Me: "I keep waking up in the middle of the night to pee; I never do that. And my belly keeps moving and it's not gas. I think I'm pregnant."

And this is where my story began. In the early morning of a cold, chilly November day, an eighteen-year-old college student discovered she was pregnant and going to have a baby.

How was I going to tell my parents? What is life going to be like? A baby? Not a teddy bear, not a toy, not a car, not a laptop, but a human being is inside me. Wait. The baby has a heartbeat, beautiful tiny hands, and feet. The baby continues to grow within me. No matter what, I am going to keep this baby. Yes. It's my responsibility and I will make it.

My name is Samantha Amaraegbu. I am the youngest daughter in a family of four kids. Even though I have a younger brother, for some odd reason, I am still considered the baby (. . . and I was having a baby). Digesting the pill that the youngest girl in the family is having a child was not easy. I had it out for me. At one point, it seemed that everyone was against me. I heard it all — the insults, the derogatory comments, the apparent shame I brought to my family. One expression really stuck with me: "Babies should not have babies." (Mind you, I was eighteen years old, not twelve).

I still get these questions today. "How are you doing it all? How do you manage everything — work, school, and your daughter?" To avoid any lectures or unsolicited advice, I usually tell people, "Oh it's okay, it's not that hard, I'm making it happen." If you really want to know, though, here goes the raw truth and nothing but the truth.

Hey teen mama, single mama, you've got this! I had this and I still do.

The day finally arrived. On July 5, 2013, my beautiful baby was born. A beautiful girl came into this world, eyes wide open. I became a mom at eighteen years old. The first day was hard. My baby wasn't with me. There was a complication in which the umbilical cord was around her neck. She stayed the night in the Neonatal Intensive Care Unit (NICU). Thankfully, it wasn't a long stay, and we were able to go home the next day.

Breastfeeding (which, by the way, was not all unicorns and rainbows the first couple times) was an overall hurtful experience. Who would have thought that one's breast could be so full that a mere arm movement can make you cry? It took me a while to get used to it, but a warm rag at these moments became my best friend. No one, and I mean no one, ever told me that breastfeeding would be painful. Another experience I lived through was the infamous stitches. *Yeah. Amazing, right? Wrong* — *one forgets how to pee or even how to shower.*

I got discharged from the hospital on a Monday. It was a beautiful hot, summer day. Here is where the challenges began. I wasn't living with my daughter's dad at the time. As a matter a fact, I never did. I often wonder whether things would be different had we lived together instead. *Would I still be with him? Would he be more involved in my daughter's life? Would I be less impatient and more understanding?*

We started off as a great couple, although my family never met him until my pregnancy. We were happy. After the baby was born, things got a little shaky. The stress of not being together twenty-four hours a day, seven days a week was draining. The build-up of feelings, of not being understood, the lack of help and presence took its toll on us and our relationship. I'm sure

I am not alone. We all picture this beautiful perfection for our lives and the lives of our children, but life rarely goes according to plan.

Things hit rock bottom, or so I thought. Our relationship was stormy every day. Thundershowers were calmer than we were. The violence, the verbal abuse, the physical abuse — it felt scary, toxic, and never-ending.

He was a smoker. All I wanted from him was to stop smoking when the baby was around and to set boundaries with his friends to do the same; if not, then at least to go outside to smoke. Let's just say that he did not take that well. Within seconds, my back was pinned to the wall and I was being shaken. Our baby had just fallen asleep. I couldn't scream or she would wake up, and putting her back to sleep would be another task. I fought back. Well, I tried to. Hitting his chest and trying to kick him off me, only for him to laugh at me, take me by the throat, and fling my body to the other side of the room. I was paralyzed, in shock. I couldn't believe it. I was scared, not for myself, but for my daughter. I had to leave her there overnight because it was really late and it was her christening the next day. We had mutually arranged for her to stay with him overnight so that I could finish the last-minute preparations without any "disturbance." My heart ached with pain, sadness, and worry. I was embarrassed. Now that I think of it, this is the first time I am sharing this incident. I knew, and I still know, if he is ever around her, that he will never hurt his own flesh and blood; however, as a mother, I feared for her well-being, for both of our well-being.

As the usual toxic relationship goes, the sweet talking, the apologies, and the false reassurances took place before I even got home. We were on the phone talking, him singing apologetic words in my ear, convincing me that everything will be all right and that it will never happen again. That is, until what I define as "the eye opener."

It was Thanksgiving. I went to the salon to get my hair styled because we had family coming over. I brought my daughter with me. She was going to spend some time with her father and his family during the day and then spend some time with my family later that evening. In the days leading up to Thanksgiving weekend, her father and I had been arguing constantly. We both thought that we would be getting married at some point; at least, that's how it had felt. I still had the rings he gifted me on my birthday. Although they were not engagement rings, they still represented a promise we made to one another.

That same Thanksgiving evening, I gave the rings back to him and told him we needed some time to really think about our futures. He put our daughter in her stroller and left her by the door. I was getting her bags ready when he turned me around and pushed me onto his bed. He jumped on me and punched me repeatedly in my stomach. It felt like the air was literally being punched out of me; I screamed and I kicked, calling for help, yet nobody heard my cries. He then continued to assault me by choking me. My eyes were tearing. I couldn't really breathe, and I kept thinking, *Am I going to die?* He pulled my pants off and raped me, and *that* is when his mother walked in, screaming about what was going on. Startled and not expecting anyone to walk in on him, he jumped right off me. I took that opportunity to grab my clothes and my stuff and get out. But before I knew it, he was behind me again. He had a pair of sharp scissors and attacked me with them. I managed to get away and finally left the building, but then his mother was now chasing me. The police were called by a passerby on the street, and that is how my Thanksgiving ended.

This incident brought on other unpleasant events, such as him stalking me and eventually assaulting me again, spitting on me, attempting to light my jacket on fire, and breaking my glasses. All in one day. This was the end for me. I guess for him as well. Something had to change, so I chose to end the relationship. Here I found my new reality — I was a nineteen-year-old single mother.

After serving time in prison, he moved to another city. I still get calls once in a while, and I encourage my daughter to speak with him and build a relationship with him because regardless of what he did to me and our tumultuous history, he is still her father.

My daughter often has episodes of sudden sadness and mourning, and she misses him. These moments are something every single mother and father must go through. These moments of profound sadness and mourning are something I still do not have a solution to, and these are moments I still struggle with. *How do I answer her questions? Should I ignore them?* One day I will know exactly what to do in these situations. But for now, I am doing my best to ensure that she is happy and does not feel alone.

Being a mother at the tender age of eighteen is also a financial burden. I was not given maternity leave, so I had to look for work as soon as I recovered postnatally. Most young mothers have to go through this. We do not have the luxury to stay home with our bundle of joy for a year. We don't have an income. We have no choice but to enroll our child(ren) in daycare (yes, this is an additional expense) at the earliest age possible. In my case, I had to put my daughter in daycare when she was six months old. My days would start at 6am and end at 10pm, on a good day. Finding a reasonable and suitable job was the biggest issue we faced. For instance, the companies always hiring are call center jobs; the hours you are most likely to be hired for from the get-go are 4pm to midnight, and there is a high probability of working on the weekends. NEXT! You get a minimum wage job and, well, the money you earn is not enough. So here comes the stress, the depression. The feeling of not being able to financially provide for your baby is extremely discouraging.

But, Mama, here is where it gets beautiful. You are strong. You are doing more than the best you can. You are doing fine. I must admit, I never heard these words before, and you may not have either. But it's okay. During my training at one of my previous jobs, my instructor told the group, "Life is like a river, and right now your boat may seem as though it is stuck, but you will soon keep rowing, since the river never ends." Thank you, Andrew (if ever you read this book) — these words motivated me every time I felt like giving up.

I wanted a better life for myself, for my baby girl. Working these odd jobs was not fun; I could barely earn enough to make ends meet. I decided then that it was time to go back to school. To be fair, I always did tell myself that I would go back to school, but juggling a baby, school, and work is extremely hard. Let's add taking care of yourself into this mix — something so important, but extremely neglected.

I began a three-year college program in paralegal studies and finally finished the program in 2018. Let me tell you, before I was even able to finish my college program, I was already being ambushed with questions about going to university. Last year was my hardest year. Anxiety, depression, and feeling lost were basically who I became. It consumed me, but I overcame it. I will go to university on my own timing. Even today, people will approach me and tell me all sorts of things — anything from "well-meaning" but unsolic-

262 YOU'VE GOT THIS, MAMA, TOO

ited advice to plain unconstructive criticism. I take it in one ear and let it out the other. This is my life, and I am in control.

Young mothers and young single mothers, your life has not ended. Your life is not ruined. Your life is just beginning. You will overcome every obstacle you face. You will be successful in everything and anything you put your mind to. People will talk. That is okay because they will do so regardless of your situation. You will want to give up, you will feel lost, and that is completely normal. Do not give up. You may not achieve your goals right away, but fight and push through despite the fear, despite the odds, and you will get there.

Here is something people tend to forget: Everybody struggles, be it financially or emotionally, be it with a child or without a child, be it single or in a relationship. Everyone hits a bump in the road. The important part is to remember to keep driving. Do not fear, do not worry that because you are doing this alone, your child may not become anything. They will. They will be bigger than you ever imagined. They will be brighter than the sun. They will shine brighter than a diamond. Why, you may ask? Because you've got this, Mama.

~A special thank you to my beautiful daughter — without you in my life, I would not have discovered my strength.

20
MY JOURNEY TO BECOMING A MOMBOSS

by Shayla Wey

"*No matter where you are in your journey, you can always redirect, Mama.*"

Shayla Wey

Shayla is a motivated MomBoss, devoted to a life of friends, family, and fitness. When not working or hanging out with her kids, you will likely find her making new friends or running marathons on the weekends. While pursuing her commerce degree at the University of Calgary, Shayla was offered a sole proprietorship with Vector Marketing that has flourished into one of the top-ranked sales offices in all of North America. Her career path was not a linear one: she experienced early success as a direct sales rep, later hired and trained hundreds of reps as the lead sales manager in her office, worked from home through the births of her two children, and is currently the District Manager of Vector Marketing Calgary. She now spends her work days mentoring the next generation of young business owners. Shayla is committed to helping people live a life that satisfies their values, which she models by being a present mom, wife, leader, and business owner. Shayla and her husband, Brad, have traveled the world with their kids, Carter and Brooklynn. She believes that consistently growing her capacity is the key to experiencing more of the amazing opportunities life has to offer with the same amount of time — when Shayla's plate gets full, she gets a bigger plate. Shayla is beyond grateful for the life she has created and is excited about the future as she continues to learn, grow, and dream.

www.mombossyyc.com
ig: @mombossyyc | @shaylawey
fb: Shayla Dupont Wey

"She believed she could, so she did."
~ R. S. Grey, Scoring Wilder

It's 6:15 am and I hear footsteps inching toward our bedroom door. The door slowly opens and in tiptoes Brooklynn, our sweet and mischievous toddler. As I pretend to keep sleeping and slowly pull the covers over my head in the hopes of fifteen more minutes of sleep, I know the odds of that happening are highly unlikely. Her little body climbs into bed and she proceeds to put her face as close as humanly possible to mine and yell, "Mom, I want a popsicle!" I take a deep breath, smile, and say to myself, *Wake up MomBoss, you're living the dream.*

It's funny how life works. When you're a kid, you can't wait to be a teenager. Then as a teenager, you long to be an adult. As an adult, you dream of getting married, buying a house, and one day hopefully becoming a mom. It all sounds so simple on paper, but just like an airplane that is off course ninety percent of the time en route to its destination, so is the case with life. Well, at least my life.

My journey of becoming a MomBoss began as a university student back in 2006 when I first walked through the doors of Vector Marketing, the exclusive distributor of CUTCO Cutlery. That day, so many chapters of my life would begin to be written. This was a direct sales position, and I remember feeling both nervous and excited. When you share with people that you just got a job selling knives, the reaction is usually one of skepticism. I always liked exploring opportunities, but this just seemed so different. My first presentation was with my parents, who had told me they weren't going to buy anything. However, they were impressed with the quality of the Cutco product, and they purchased a set. Even though my first customers were my parents, I will never forget the feeling of that first sale. Little did I know that sale would be the beginning of a journey that would change my life forever.

That first summer, my main motivation to sell was to get some experience that would look good on my resume. As my success continued, I quickly advanced into management training in the fall and was a leading sales representative for the company while pursuing my Bachelor of Commerce at the University of Calgary full-time. I would go on to win multiple sales-based scholarships, trophies, and trips to various places in the world. Who would have thought my job selling knives would provide so many amazing experiences!

I graduated in April 2009 and was married a couple months later in November. Our wedding was at the Banff Springs Hotel, and it was beautiful — family, friends, and even a little bit of snow. When the wedding was over, I had a moment when I thought I should now get a big girl job and start the next chapter of my life.

Focus areas I wanted in my so-called "big girl job" included:

- Flexibility (not nine-to-five)
- Love the people I work with
- Growth opportunities (personal & professional)
- Good money
- Travel

After compiling the list, I realized that I already had all these things in my current role with Vector. My focus shifted to pursuing my career at Vector for the next couple of years. With this new focus, my success with the organization increased dramatically. My mentor, Angie Macdougall, selected me to be her pilot sales manager; we set many records that still stand a decade later, and I was only in my mid-twenties.

The success I experienced allowed me and my husband to travel around the world. We were able to have the wedding of our dreams, build our first home, shop at our leisure, dine out, and enjoy so many of the little things that life has to offer.

Soon I was ready for the next chapter of our lives: babies! As much as I was "ready" (or thought I was), nothing can truly prepare you for the emotions that you go through during this stage of life. To say that getting pregnant is an emotional journey is a true understatement: from counting target days to asking Dr. Google every question that pops in your brain to being excited-and-then-freaking-out . . . all within a five minute span! What a roller coaster season.

Perhaps you know exactly where you were when the stick showed two lines . . .

. . . when the doctor confirmed you were expecting

. . . when you saw a little heartbeat at eight weeks

. . . and then again at twelve weeks!

Finally, we were ready to share the news with our family and friends: Baby Wey was coming in June!

I grew up with the most incredible group of ladies a girl could ask for. Most of my close friends weren't in the baby stage of life yet, though, so I went through a lot of my pregnancy journey feeling scared of the unknown. I am a planner, and not knowing what to expect next freaked me out.

Was the baby going to be a boy or girl? Would I be a good mom? What was my work going to think? Would I go back to work? So many questions!

I remember sharing some of my concerns about work with another mentor, Joe Cardillo, who was then the national sales manager. His response was, "You've never had a baby, you've never been a mom. One thing I will tell you is that no matter what you decide when you come back, you will have a choice of roles here. Think of it like choosing between a Porsche, Mercedes, or BMW; there are so many positions you would be great at, don't worry, it will all work out." That conversation really stuck with me over the years, and I still believe it to be true today. In life, there are always options; it's up to you as to which one you pursue.

June 30 came quickly, and Carter William entered this world. I was a mommy. After I got settled into my new routine of feedings, diaper changes, and endless snuggles, I started to feel bored. *A feeling no new mom should feel, right?* I started seeking out things to fill my days but felt like I never seemed to accomplish anything. As much as I tried to just "be" and enjoy the moments, I was getting restless. I started to think about how my professional life would look now that I was a mom.

Could I still have a successful career? Could I still "love what I do" and be a good mom?

I didn't think it would be possible to return to my previous position and still be a good mom (which I found out later was not true). So at only three months postpartum, I went back to the drawing board. I wrote down a list of all of the things I wanted in my next chapter of life. Interestingly, the list still looked like this:

- Flexibility (not nine-to-five)
- Love the people I work with
- Growth opportunities (personal & professional)
- Make money
- Travel

Although the list was precisely the same as before, it now had a different meaning.

Around this time, a role opened up within Vector: National Sales Promotion Manager. I already loved the company and the culture, and I wanted to stay. I knew this job would be a perfect fit, my next dream job. One challenge: The placement was in Oakville, Ontario, and we were committed to building our family in Calgary.

However, I am a firm believer that if things are meant to be, they will work out. So I applied for the position and was interviewed a couple of times. I was asked questions like:

"How would this work if you live in Calgary?"

"How would you make this work around a three-month-old baby?"

"Why do you think this is a good fit for you?"

Confidently, I responded, "I would find a way to make it work."

As much as I knew I wanted to stay at Vector, it turns out they wanted me to stay, too: I got the job! I was pumped. I now had something to do when Carter was napping!

The transition into the new role was pretty smooth, as I was able to work from home. This meant early mornings, productive nap times, and late nights. I felt like I had a bigger purpose again than "just being a mom," which made me feel like I was a better mom. I always describe my life as a puzzle. Pieces of my puzzle include my husband, my kids, my family, my friends, my fitness, and my career. In many ways, having this final puzzle piece — a new career track I was excited about — made me feel complete. I needed to stop feeling guilty and own the fact that my career, in addition to being a mom, was what I needed to feel fulfilled, and that was okay.

In 2015, we were blessed with a little girl, Brooklynn Jean. I never imagined that my heart could grow bigger, but it did. Both of our kids' genders were a surprise so when she arrived, it was a pink explosion in our house. Our family of four was complete.

Going from one to two kids was a bit of an adjustment. I knew we weren't planning on having more kids, so this time I made the decision to slow things down and enjoy a full one-year maternity leave (well, almost a full year). Our year was full of laughs, tears, smiles, meltdowns, play dates, lots of coffee, and some wine, too!

As my maternity leave was coming to an end, I started thinking about transitioning back into my sales promotion role. I was excited to get back to work and find that balance that everyone wants. I knew working from home with two kids would be more of a challenge, so we decided that sending the kids to a day home part-time would make the most sense to allow me some time to work during normal hours. I was so fortunate to make my schedule work around my son, so the thought of sending my second to a day home (even if it was only part-time) didn't sit well with me. I went back and forth about whether or not this was the best decision and whether I was a bad mom because of it. But I remembered reading *Lean In* by Sheryl Sandberg a few years ago, in which she referenced that women need to look at childcare as an investment in their career. This really resonated with me and eventually gave me the confidence that I was making the right decision.

We got into our new groove and after about a year back in my role, I realized I was entering another chapter of life. The "we're done having kids" phase. That was it, this was it. Five years just flew by! So much of what I worked hard for and achieved was here, and I was beyond grateful to take on this new adventure of life.

As this new chapter opened, I realized it was time to go back to the drawing board. This is the list I came up:

- Flexibility (not nine-to-five)
- Love the people I work with
- Growth opportunities (personal & professional)
- Make Money
- Travel

Again, it was the same list, but the points had come to have different meanings.

I did some career searching outside of Vector and found some things I would succeed in, but questions lingered in my mind. *What if I became a district executive and owned my own business in Calgary for Vector Marketing? What if I actually did well? What if I could build an empire to have a life in which I could continue to learn, grow, and dream? I guess I would never know unless I gave it a shot, right?*

The decision to open up my own business was not an easy one. Although I had years of experience in the business, I still never believed enough in myself. It's a weird thing to experience success on so many levels but then still doubt yourself. I wanted all the things owning a business offered but was scared of what it would take to get there.

"How would I run a business and still be a good mom?"

"Could I still make time for my husband?"

"What about all of my friends?"

"And working out?"

"When would I have time for groceries?

". . . and laundry?"

". . . and walking the dog?"

". . . and . . ."

The list continued.

As my list of fears grew, I needed to remind myself of *why* this would be good for me. I needed a clear vision of what I wanted in this next chapter of life.

After multiple conversations with my husband, close friends, and myself, I decided to take the leap on August 1, 2017. I was doing it. I was opening up my own office for Vector Marketing and would be a MomBoss. This would be my new definition of me. The transition from working from home to now owning a business in downtown Calgary was a big one. But in my moments of weakness, my *why* was strong enough to keep me moving forward.

The transition was emotional at first. There was the fulfillment of knowing I was going after a dream, as well as the satisfaction that I had finally committed; however, there were also the fears, the doubts, and the mom guilt. Oh, the mom guilt. Dropping off my kids in the early morning left me in tears, some days questioning if I had made the right decision.

The first month went by quickly and as I got into my new routine, the doubts and fears started to lessen and I started believing in myself more. As the belief in myself grew, so did my business. The more exciting my life got *outside* of the business, the better things were *in* my business. My definition of success is not just how much my business sells or how many people I recruit or how much money I make. **Success is defined by *how* I can find a way to incorporate everything that is important to me, all while enjoying the journey.**

As my business grew, I knew I needed to set up a schedule I was excited about. I made a list of things that were important to me and no matter how busy I get with work, these things are crucial to my success.

First on that list was me. What did I need to ensure I was healthy and happy to be the best MomBoss possible? It might sound odd to think of putting yourself first, but I knew that if I could be the best version of me, then my marriage would be better and if my marriage was solid, our kids would be better because of that. It was a domino effect. How we are in one area of life is how we are in all areas of life.

So what would it take to keep me healthy and happy? Working out and some alone time. Pretty simple, but important. I needed to schedule time for my workouts. When I am working out, I feel stronger. With strength comes confidence and better decisions throughout my day. I needed that. Lots of it. I have created a schedule that allows me to have some time for me. Some days that means 6am spin classes, other days it's a 9pm run; on the weekends the kids come along with me so I can make my favourite class, Body Pump. This is a juggling act with my work schedule, my husband's work schedule, and the kids' activities, but it is important to me so I make it happen.

The second thing I love about being a MomBoss and creating my own schedule is our weekly date night. I am a bit obsessed with the concepts in Gary Chapman's book, *The Five Love Languages* (great read, a relationship game-changer!). My husband's primary love language is quality time; mine is acts of service (although Brad does seem to think I have a list of about nine love languages). We make it a priority to go on a date night almost every Wednesday, and this has become one of our favourite nights of the week. I think it is important that we invest the time and money into our relationship. I find a way to pay my cell phone bill each month, so why wouldn't we invest in our marriage?

Third is my kids: being a MomBoss has also helped me prioritize the time I spend with them. I have been able to cultivate *quality time* over *quantity*. Finding the right balance isn't easy, but one-on-one time with each of my kids has been something I have enjoyed so much. The more I worked through the transition of being away, the more I cherished the time with my kids. I set my schedule up so that every Wednesday is my day with my kids. I get to spend time with both of them right in the middle of my week! It's easy to get caught up in associating a feeling with each day of the week, and I am continually working against the norm.

The fourth consideration is my girl squad. My girlfriends have always been my biggest cheerleaders, supporters, and the ones to celebrate all of life's moments with. As I was navigating my career path, the girls have always been there to believe in me every step of the way. I am blessed to have such incredible women in my life. They help me be a better MomBoss.

Real life is crazy. When I pause to think about my journey thus far, I never thought I would be where I am. As I build my empire as a district executive, my job is so much more than a title. The decision to become a MomBoss came from wanting to help other people go after their dreams, too. As an athlete, you have an opportunity to become a five-star recruit, with everyone wanting you on his or her team. My goal in my business is to help young adults become a five-star recruit in life. I get the opportunity to teach my team goal-setting skills, time management, how to handle rejection, public speaking, sales skills, and how to dream big. Vector has been the vehicle in my life that's helped me pursue my dreams. I get to be a MomBoss to so many people who have never had a good coach or mentor or even parent who believed in them. I get to do that every day.

I mentioned earlier that when an airplane is en route to a destination, it is off course ninety percent of the time. Life is the same. No matter where you are in your mom journey, know that you can always re-direct your path. Go do you! I'm here to tell you that you are enough, you can do it, and you will inspire more people than you know. The world needs more MomBoss leaders.

It's 7:30 pm and Carter and Brooklynn have picked out their stories. We read, we sing a few songs, I ask them what they are grateful for and tell them why I love them. The day has been long and adventurous, but now it's time to say goodnight. After they are asleep, I take a deep breath and tackle the laundry, prep some meals, check my email, maybe have a bath, and enjoy a glass of wine.

You've Got this, MomBoss!

~Thank you to my parents for encouraging me to dream big. Thank you to my husband, Brad, who loves and supports me in every way possible. My kiddos, Carter and Brooklynn, you are a dream come true. My girlsquad is the best ever — love you ladies! My mentors Angie and Joe — thanks for believing in me. To everyone else who makes up my village, I appreciate you!

21
BLISS IN THE CHAOS

by Lisa Aamot

" *. . . But in the chaos, there is always bliss to be found.* "

Lisa Aamot

Lisa Marie Aamot grew up in the Pacific Northwest near Seattle, WA. From a young age, books captivated her and she knew she wanted to become a writer. She completed her B.A. in human development with a certification in early childhood development from Washington State University. After having her son, and with the support of her high school sweetheart and husband of eight years, Kyle, she decided to pursue her passion in photography so she could spend more time at home. She is now a published award-winning photographer and proud owner of Meraki Photography NW. She credits motherhood for the way she captures life in all seasons. Having her son opened her eyes to the blissful chaos of parenthood. She began sharing her experiences of motherhood before noon in between cups of reheated coffee on social media. Lisa believes that motherhood is holy work and that it contains the greatest magic in even the smallest moments.

In 2017, while pregnant with her daughter, her life took a scary turn. After fighting Cytomegalovirus, she learned that it had passed through the placenta and their battle was just beginning. As she faces the unknowns of her daughter's diagnosis, she is using her social media platform to spread awareness about CMV and childhood hearing loss. Through this journey, she has learned to believe in the power of the village and to lean on women both near and far for support.

www. merakiphotographynw.com
Ig: @lisaaamot

"It was her chaos that made her beautiful." ~ Atticus

I already know what I'll miss most when I'm eighty years old. That pitter patter of tiny little feet in the morning. Discovering the blissful chaos of motherhood, and this season of life that is toddlers and babies. These years in which I'm growing my village and we are soaking in all the tears and joy together.

There are two kinds of pitter-pattering feet with toddlers. There's the kind that ends with a tiny human staring you down from the edge of your bed — I refer to this as the *Children of the Corn* stare. Then there's the kind that is quick, then slow as it passes the door, then quick, then silent. This is the pitter patter that wakes me from the deepest sleep.

The first time I experienced the "Get up immediately, who cares what the neighbors see!" pitter patter was when our daughter, Kinley, was a few months old and our son, Mason, was the blessed age of two and a half. I turned the corner of our living room to see tiny powdery footprints in a trail across our entire house. They led me to the happiest toddler in the world, sitting smack in the middle of five pounds of pancake mix. He informed me that I could "just go to the store and get more." I remember thinking, later that day, how I wished I had just sat with him and savored that moment. That I had drawn pictures in the mix on the floor or grabbed some toy cars and played with him before cleaning it up. I wish I had realized in the beginning of that moment that the chaos can be bliss.

Too often we spend our days just getting by. We laugh about the re-heated coffee and dream about the wine waiting for us to drink it once an acceptable hour hits. If I could go back, knowing what I know now, I would soak in every ounce of the bliss. Even on the hardest, or in this case messiest, days, there is so much bliss to be found in motherhood.

The truth is that in the months leading up to the "pancake incident," we were maxed out on chaos. It never would have crossed my mind to see bliss in any of it. Our world started to flip upside-down when I told my obstetrician (OB) at thirty-one weeks pregnant that I felt like something was very wrong. I could feel it deep in my core.

Almost two weeks later, with worsening symptoms and no one believing my hormonal, round-bellied self, I was laying on my couch in the middle of the night with tears streaming down my face. I could not move from the pain. All I could think about was all the moments of Mason's life I was sure I would miss. My chest tightened, and I could feel the panic setting in. I was trying not to go down the dark hole of WebMD or Google. I could see his journal across the room, and I wanted to will myself to get up and write letters to him for each of those moments I wouldn't be there for. The pain kept me from moving, though, so I grabbed my phone and texted my friend Jaylin. I told her I thought I was dying, and I genuinely meant it. We joke about this any time we have the smallest ailment, but this time was different. It felt overwhelmingly real. In the middle of a dark night, the village reached out and whispered "I got you" in the form of a simple text from my friend. She told me I would be okay, but also validated my fear. She reassured me to trust my gut and push for answers.

The next week was a whirlwind of endless tests and overwhelming in-formation. They rushed me in an ambulance to the University of Washington labor and delivery in Seattle, where we learned that I was in preterm labor and that several of my organs were being attacked by something unknown.

Our daughter stayed put, but a few days later, the doctors came in donning masks and paper gowns. I thought for sure I had some apocalyptic virus. I was going to give birth to a zombie. They diagnosed me with Cytomega-lovirus (CMV).

Never heard of it? I hadn't either. They told us that "primary" would be the worst-case scenario and that it would be unlikely because roughly eighty-five percent of people have contracted CMV by adulthood.

I wasn't most people.

The onslaught of unknowns and what ifs was just the beginning. No one warned me to brace myself for the chaos that was about to consume our lives.

I didn't realize it at the time, but my village was trying desperately to help me find the little joys and moments of small bliss even in this storm. One of my best friends, Danielle, brought me a smoothie and made me smile when my body was trying to shut down on me. I couldn't tell you what we talked about, but I know that it was a bright spot. I had so much magnesium pumping through me that I had been hallucinating most of that day. Having her there calmed me down. Some people just feel like home, and I needed to feel that. To breathe and get out of my head. A couple days later, my best friend from college, Ashlee, hopped on a ferry just to sit with me while Kyle (my husband) went home to be with Mason for a night. She didn't have to show up, but she did. We put on those silly masks and paper gowns so she could jailbreak me from my hospital room. She made me forget the pain and scary unknowns for a few hours. We laughed so hard I was sure Kinley would just fall out on the floor. We renamed all the residents based on whom they most resembled from *Greys Anatomy*. Just like the show, every time a doctor came in, a whole swarm of residents followed them. That's a lot of eyes on my lady tunnel!

As the afternoon ended, Ashlee offered to stay the night with me so I wouldn't be alone, but I told her I would be fine. The second the door closed, I fell apart. Something burst in me. I sobbed and couldn't breathe. All the fear and anxiety bubbled over. It was a strange mixture of panic and release. Maybe I needed to give myself permission to fall apart, but a part of me will always regret not saying yes to her when I needed her. Why do we do that? Push our village away when they are standing right there ready to be leaned on, basically shouting to us, "I'm here, lean on me!" During that week, I only felt the heaviness of motherhood. Looking back, I see my village surrounding me and pointing out the tiny moments of joy that are there even in the pain.

Kinley was born a little over a month after we left the hospital. We watched our tiny human get poked and prodded. The CMV had crossed through the placenta, so instead of soaking in our new baby, we were shuffling her around from one appointment to the next. She spent a day with swollen eyes from having them tested and manually maneuvered. She spent countless hours hooked up to wires in the hearing clinic. CMV is the leading non-genetic cause of childhood hearing loss, and learning this could happen at any point until age six was devastating.

The chaos of those first months consumed me. All the unknowns and what if's kept me awake at night. It was all I saw, and it was draining. Cytomegalovirus was new to us. I thought it was rare. Contrary to my assumption, however, I learned it affects 1:150 newborns. Every single hour in the United States, a child is permanently disabled from CMV. [3]

I didn't understand why I wasn't warned. If it was so common, why hadn't I been informed? Even some of the obstetricians and doctors we met with couldn't answer our questions about this virus. With each appointment, we heard new or different information, and my heart was aching to know how to advocate for our baby girl.

No one warns you about motherhood being lonely, but I felt so alone during this time. I knew that I had to lean on my village or I would drown, but I couldn't bring myself to do it. My mother surrounded us with the most incredibly strong women. I watched as they shared this beautiful give-and-take. From making meals to watching each other's children, they walked through life together. A village raised me, so why was it so hard for me to tell them that I needed them?

I called my mother's best friend Sandy my "Aunt." Her family was our family. Sandy's oldest daughter, Ginger, was my second mom. Now I know she took on that role because it was what they had shown her through our mother's sisterhood. The bond our moms shared was so strong it spoke volumes. I had no idea we weren't actually related to Sandy and her family until an embarrassing age. That was part of the beauty of the village surrounding me through my childhood. My mom and her small village of women would drop us off at school and jump in each other's cars to grab a coffee or finally eat a hot meal. I imagine a lot of mornings were spent at the mall. They said they were mall walking, but now I know that is just faking exercise while actually shopping.

---

3   Newborn Screening. (n.d.). Retrieved from https://www.nationalcmv.org/congenital-cmv/newborn-screening

Even before I had Mason, I knew I wanted to have a village like this. I wanted my children to be surrounded in its magic, too. So why did I struggle to say "yes" to mine now? I couldn't share my days because they all felt overwhelming while I was adjusting to having two humans to keep alive (well, three, if you count Kyle). To add to that, we had all of Kinley's unknowns; if I couldn't have my questions about her diagnosis answered, how could I answer everyone else's questions about it? I didn't want to burden anyone.

The morning Mason dumped the pancake mix, I let my chaos show. I took a few photos and posted them to social media. I was exhausted, but I wanted to say to the other moms who would see my post, "Hey, see this absolute mess? This is a short season, and even if you are overwhelmed by the mess, let's stop and laugh together. Me, too." I realized something so valuable on that day; no matter how far away your village is, they'll reach out if you let them.

I think I believed a village had to be women who share the same street name as you, or at least the same zip code. After all, the village my mother created were all so close — in proximity and in heart. It was what I knew. I didn't see my village right in front of me because they all felt so far. But they found me that day by sharing their stories of chaos with me and helping me see the beauty in the mess my son had made. Looking back, my village showed up when we were first starting our journey with CMV, too — by text, through Seattle rush hour traffic, and by boat. They showed up.

If we open ourselves up to our village, we will find it's so much bigger than we ever knew. It's not just the friends we see in our day-to-day lives. It's the women who are there to encourage, laugh, or even cry with us. The village is boundless if you allow it to be. They are there to help us dig out the silver linings and to melt the fear or anxiety away so the joy can bubble up and out of us again. Sometimes they are the women who sit with us in our worry. Other times, they are there to remind us to be present even in the long days of motherhood. They are the women who help us shake off our mom pants and remind us who we are underneath the spit up stains. They are the women who say, "I see you still."

After I cleaned up most of the pancake mix and posted the photos, my phone rang. MOM. I contemplated not answering because I was exhausted from dealing with the biggest mess my pantry had ever seen, and probably a blowout or two from Kinley by that hour. I answered it. She was laughing. She was laughing at my post and called to tell me how funny she found my predicament. I wasn't annoyed, because I knew deep down that it was funny. I was trying so hard to be okay with the chaos and embrace it by being open about it with my post.

Then the woman who taught me about the importance of the village and the holy work of motherhood told me something profound. She told me that one of her favorite memories from motherhood was a completely chaotic and messy moment just like the one I was probably still cleaning up (which I was). She said at the time it never would have occurred to her to take a photo, but of all the moments she had captured, she wished she had captured that blissful chaos. A moment when two of her sons were found surrounded in broken eggs, flour, and milk, trying to surprise her with breakfast in bed. It was a season of life she loved so much, but that had passed too quickly.

Those words hit me in a strange way. "Blissful chaos" kept repeating in my head. *Can those two words really coexist in the same moment?* Then I realized she was right about her memory. Her story of chaos had so much bliss in it. It was a season of life she cherished. That season of little pitter-pattering feet running to give the biggest hugs or sneaking off to create the biggest innocent mess. It was stories like that one that she shared with her village during mall walks and lunch dates. I looked at the mess at my feet and the happy toddler still playing in it. I thought to myself *Yeah, it kind of was a blissful morning with Mason in the pantry.*

In that moment, I was glad I shared it and glad my village could see the beautiful mess I found myself in and help me laugh about it.

Motherhood is chaos. Over the last year, though, I've learned to soak it all in, because someday when I look back on this, that's where I'll find the bliss. Smack dab in the middle of a five-pound powdery mess on the floor. My perfect baby boy beaming up at me, declaring I can just go get more pancake mix at the store. We did get more pancake mix. Life kept going, and messes kept happening. My heart opened up to the simple joys. I shared my worries and anxiety surrounding Kinley having CMV, but even in that, my village has helped me find silver linings.

At the beginning of our journey, I couldn't see the village of women standing there ready to be leaned on. Now I know to not only reach for my village, but also to be that person for them even if they are silent. *Especially* when they are silent. Because in the pain, in the worry, in the long days of motherhood, we feel the chaos. But in the chaos, there is always bliss to be found. No matter how near or far, surround yourself with a village of women who will laugh with you, cry with you, and soak it all in with you.

~I would like to thank my husband, Kyle, for supporting me through this process. Mason and Kinley, thank you for all the bliss and chaos you bring to my life on a daily basis. My village, both past and present, for being strong women I can look to. And last but not least, Mr. Protzeller, because when I was an awkward teenage girl, you believed in me and told me one day I would be a published author.

FINAL THOUGHTS

FEATURING

Sabrina Greer and Elaine Kaley

In closing, I wanted to share this space with someone who has been through it all and come out the other side. I wanted to speak to a recovering perfectionist. A mama who could really breathe some life into the ideologies discussed throughout this book. Someone with lots of experience and time in the *mama game*. In *You've Got This, Mama*, I co-authored the closing notes with my mama, Linda Greer. This worked really well. It was incredibly eye-opening and powerful. The world loved hearing from a warrior who went before us. They enjoyed knowing that while things are, of course, wildly different now in terms of social media, technology, and day-to-day life, the emotions attached to motherhood are identical. The centuries, decades, and generations may have changed, evolved differently from each other, but at the heart of it all, the spirit, soul, and very emotion of motherhood still remains the same.

When I thought about who would be a good fit to coauthor the closing notes of this book, it was easy. Elaine is the mother of my best friend. She has been a huge influence and maternal figure in my life. Having such a powerful maternal figure in my life in addition to my own mother has been a great blessing, and one I covet more than she knows. She is a counselor, specializing in relationships and self-love. She has two children of her own and is now a grandmother to five grandbabies. Rather than trying to ghostwrite and summarize our interview and dozens of chats, I requested she share her story, in her words. And so she did . . .

"And they lived happily ever after," If only that were so . . .

The **perfect** husband, the **perfect** home, the **perfect** child — I had what I like to call "A Cinderella Complex." Always striving for perfection. Worried about pleasing everyone else.

I grew up in a far-from-perfect home. My mom was an only child and attended church every Sunday; my dad was a handsome, beer-drinking, hangout-with-the-boys kind of guy, and my maternal grandmother lived with us. It was for sure a rather chaotic environment. Very early on in life, due to my "need to please" and perfectionist nature, I started envisioning my perfect life. I would marry a handsome, six-foot-tall, blue-eyed man with blond hair. We would have two beautiful children and we WOULD live happily ever after. I read every book I could find on how to have a happy marriage and, soon after, on how to be a perfect mother. I would do it perfectly with God's help.

Then came June 2, 1979 at 5:14pm when I heard my husband announce after twelve hours of "natural" childbirth, "We have our boy." Of course we had a boy. I had prayed specifically for a "blue-eyed, blond hair, fat-cheeked baby boy." I had, and continue to have, very simple faith and was taught that we need to be specific in our prayer life. Here was the perfect answer to my prayers. Ben Alden Kaley: 9 lbs, 14 ozs. He arrived eight days early, according to **plan** — *well, my plan.*

The night before this life-changing experience, I cleaned my house, made a batch of cookies, checked on the beautiful nursery in my custom-built home, and went to bed feeling certain I would deliver the next day, and I did.

I was going to breastfeed (not popular at that time), use cloth diapers (better for my baby and more economical,) and he would sleep for four hours, awake, and happily breastfeed as I snuggled him and sang *Jesus Loves Me* and prayed he would have a happy, healthy life.

Oh, and I forgot — I would leave the hospital dressed in my pre-pregnancy clothing to return to my perfectly organized home.

"Your baby appears to have a startle complex," the nurse stated as she brought my baby to me in my hospital room. In 1979, we stayed in the hospital for three days before returning home.

"What exactly is a *startle complex*?"

My precious little guy (I was totally and absolutely in love) was definitely not comfortable out of mummy's belly. He couldn't seem to latch, he was losing weight and woke up constantly, crying and seemingly startled, often out of a deep sleep. He was jaundiced and not doing so well.

In the midst of congratulations, gifts, flowers, and visitors, I was sinking. *What had I done wrong?* The nurse was asking if I had any trauma during my pregnancy. The truth was, I had. My mom and dad had gone through a very rough patch in their marriage. I had always been the family "manager," and this all happened during the months of my pregnancy. My dad actually left home on the day of my church baby shower. I worked as an administrative assistant at our church at that time, and they had blessed me beyond measure. What should have been a joyful experience was clouded and grey. My dad, my pillar and best friend, had left. My mom was devastated, and I felt like I needed to assume full responsibility to "fix" this situation. *Was he safe? Was he coming back?* There were no cell phones to connect with or text each other at that time.

Had my concerns and fear for my dad and mom and their troubles created anxiety in my precious boy?

The nurse's question brought feelings of inadequacy and guilt. I wasn't doing well with breastfeeding either, and I felt like my *perfectly* planned world of motherhood was crumbling.

I arrived home a few days later, feeling somewhat more positive. Yes, feeling optimistic, in spite of the fact that my summer skirt would not zip up all the way or that I had very leaky breasts that were sore from trying to breastfeed and I had to sit on a blowup tube because I had so many stitches. I felt like I had it perfectly altogether. My mom and dad were doing well and had built a new home very close and were available to help. My husband was doing everything he could as well, and I was very optimistic that things would turn around.

About a week later, I put Ben down for a nap. I fed him and hoped he would sleep for four hours. In my perfect world, that is what he was supposed to do. I actually put on my pre-pregnancy two-piece bathing suit and thought I could sit in the sun for a bit. As I was about to go outside, I heard "the cry." Maybe he just needed to be changed. As I lifted his little legs and removed his diaper, he shot out a load of "__it" that landed directly in my face and down my bathing-suit-clad body. At that very moment, my dad and my husband showed up — it was lunch time — and thought it was hilariously funny. I began sobbing, and couldn't stop. I told them that it wasn't funny and I could not do this, and I quote, "This is not for today and tomorrow, this is for EIGHTEEN years."

My husband in his calm, practical manner, stated, "I am pretty sure he won't be "sh—ing" on you when he is eighteen." But I did not see the humor in this situation at all and felt so certain that my next eighteen years would be spent cleaning up baby poop explosions.

That first year was filled with so much trial and error. Breastfeeding just did not work for Ben and me. He was losing weight, and I was miserably sore. We began formula feeding, and then he had colic. Sleepless nights, walking up and down stairs to get him to burp, having him sleep on his daddy's belly to sooth his little gassy belly, and wondering if life would ever be normal again. I read, asked for advice, prayed, and listened to everyone who was *more than willing* to tell me what was best for my baby. Thankfully, by the time Ben was three months old, things got better. We now know he was lactose intolerant like his Dad, and his "startle complex" is quite likely more personality than situational.

That first year continued to have its ups and downs. Ben literally never slept past 6am, and I was *not* (and am still not) a morning person — but I was in love. Inexplicable, lay-my-life-on-the-line kinda love. Ben had literally filled my heart with a love I never knew possible. I have always loved deeply, but this precious little guy with those gorgeous big blue eyes, blond hair like corn silk, and a smile that would make anyone feel like the most important person in the world had changed my life completely.

I wish I could say that this experience changed my perfectionist nature and I approached my second child with no expectations. Jenny was completely different. She *loved* to sleep, needed a schedule, and breastfed perfectly five minutes after delivery. How does this happen? Had I finally waved a magic wand and become the "perfect mother", or are some babies just easier because of their nature? I think a bit of both.

I am now a registered social worker in New Brunswick, Canada. I have studied personalities and human behavior extensively. What have I learned?

Motherhood is one of the greatest experiences I feel a woman can ever experience. It is wonderful, tiring, exhilarating, frustrating, time-consuming, and beautiful all wrapped up in one little body. Motherhood does not come with a manual. Every child is unique. We seek advice and if you are like me, we want to do it "perfectly." I have learned there is no "perfect" parent and there is no "perfect" child. We are human, and humans are not perfect. Life is a journey. We are each writing our own story of life. At birth, we don't get to pick our parents, and we, as parents, do not get to pick our kids. They are intricately formed in our body with their own look and personality. They don't always follow our plan or fit in our *box*. No, let me reword that — they *rarely* follow our plan. I believe they are fearfully and wonderfully made by God to walk their own path in life. As parents, we have been entrusted with the awesome responsibility to prepare them for this journey.

It took me years to figure out that I did not have to do this perfectly.

Jenny, my daughter, had just graduated from high school when I decided to further my education and go to university to pursue a degree in social work. My son was engaged to be married. I am sad to say I was still very proud to be a perfectionist. I truly desired to do life right, and right meant perfect . . . perfect according to my definition. I am thankful that I did not put this definition on others, especially my children. I always encouraged them to do their best, but realized that their best may not always be an A+ in every subject or every sport. However, the bar was still set *very* high for myself, especially in motherhood.

One would think that as our children become *adults*, motherhood might get easier. Our precious little "bundles of joy" start grabbing the pen from our hands, and guess what happens?

They want to be authors of their own life story. Without question, this "tug of war" for control of their own destiny has been going on probably for years, but that milestone year of sixteen, or perhaps eighteen, now heralds the arrival of adulthood, which signifies independence. As I watched my two grown children write the chapters of their now adult life, I was not prepared for the flood of emotions that ensued. My house felt so empty. Ben had gotten married and moved into his own home, starting a new life with his beautiful, lovely bride. Jenny had moved to Toronto to follow her dreams. My house felt empty and cavernous. I filled my days with education and fulling my dream of completing my degree and starting a private counseling practice.

One year after my graduation, my world was again changed forever. I was going to be a grandmother! Oh the excitement, the dreams, and the expectations! My beautiful boy, now a handsome six-foot-and-four-inch tall young man, was going to be a dad. I honestly thought I would burst with excitement. Oh, and of course, I would be the *perfect* grandmother.

On October 6, 2005, our first grandchild arrived. She was perfectly beautiful and healthy. Here was the continuation of the little Kaley family that we had started twenty-four years ago. Many say being a grandparent is having the best of both worlds — loving deeply, enjoying the fun times, and then giving them back. However, another reality I feel is loving so very deeply but not being a part of their day-to-day, or sometimes weekly or monthly, lives. It is really a different reality, and as deeply as a grandparent's love goes, those grandbabies are the responsibility of someone else, even if that someone else is your son or daughter. As a counsellor, I hear many life stories. I have heard wonderful grandparent stories, as well as some that are just so very sad.

I am now the grandmother of five beautiful grandchildren. How do I describe this experience? Surreal, exciting, and with the sudden realization that old age is approaching, or maybe the reality that it has already arrived. It's having visions of Christmas mornings all gathered around the beautiful Christmas tree, or maybe the deep realization that your grandchild lives many miles away and is growing up without you. I have experienced some of all of the above.

Mama, Grandma, you've got this, too! Mamas grow up to be grandmas, and guess what? They need a village, too! What I have realized on my journey is this — while perfection is enticing, it is unrealistic. We must lean into the unknown, embrace the imperfections, and give in to life as it reveals its lessons. I am not a perfect mother, nor am I a perfect grandmother, but I love our imperfect lives, our imperfect family, and wouldn't change a thing.

❦ ❦ ❦

So, there you have it. The evolution of the perfectionist. Guess what, Mama? None of us are perfect, and striving for perfection is like jumping in the deepest part of the ocean with two-ton weights attached to your ankles. We do not belch rainbows and fart glitter. We are all part of this human experience. Life is an eternal journey out to sea. Some days will be smooth sailing, while some other days may feel like you are weathering crazy storms through turbulent waters. Some days will be full of adventure and fun, and others will be rocky and you will surely toss your cookies. Let the stories in this book be your life preservers and the voices, your beacon, your lighthouse.

I'm sorry if you were hoping for definitive answers, if you were thinking I had some magic spell that would make it all easier. I don't. Motherhood will mess with your compass, throw your path off track, but it's worth it. The beauty we see on our excursion is what life is all about.

Perfectionism is fear. Fear of not belonging. Fear of being judged or shamed. Fear of what others will think or say. And fear of what you think about yourself. Mamas, we need to stand together and work together to diminish this fear. If we follow the lessons learned throughout this book, it will surely be a step in the right direction.

Surrender. Let go of the idea of perfection; it is not real. We are perfectly imperfect just the way we are, and the sooner we learn to embrace this, we will be one step closer to living an authentic life.

Acceptance: Accepting what cannot be changed is a massive step toward living an authentic life. Be grateful for what you have, rather than wishing things were different.

Vulnerability: Sharing our stories with others empowers not only us but also the people listening.

Be Present: Enjoy life as it is, not as it was or should be. Embrace the past and allow it to shape you, but not define you. Move forward and write your own future.

So, Mama, no matter the stage or season of motherhood you're currently in, no matter the trials and the tribulations, you are enough. Your very quirks, your mood swings, your love for every moment — the good, the bad, the ugly — the painstakingly long hours you put into ensuring every milestone, every party, the endless attention to detail, all the sleepless nights, the mental workload that seems never-ending, your grace through the grittiness that can sometimes be motherhood — all this is what makes you so special, so irreplaceable, so *you*. Choose to give yourself that grace, choose to surrender to each moment, each smile, each cry, each giggle, and yes, each explosion of toys or even poopy diapers. Choose to accept yourself in all your glory, because your family will love you for it. Choose openness and vulnerability, because the strongest village is built not on defenses and judgements but rather on sharing, listening, and truly feeling for one another, with one another.

Choose to be present, in this very moment, because *that* is all we have — so hug and kiss those kiddos a little longer, let them help you around the house (even if it is a bit messy or not "perfect"), show them what a day in their Mama's life looks like, and maybe, just maybe, take a break and go live a day in the life of your kid! You'll be surprised at how much wisdom those tiny but mighty souls hold.

Our future moments, memories, experiences are all shaped by what we choose to do and who we choose to be in our present moment. Choose love and kindness, undying, unrelenting love and kindness, because that will see you through some sheer madness and give you the gift of abundance in ways you never thought possible. Choose you, your littles, your intuition, your heart, because before you know it, this, too, shall pass. And if ever in doubt, I want you to know that you have a sister in every woman in this book, in this series — we are here, we see you, and we've definitely got you! You've got this, Mama, you most definitely have!

~ To every single imperfect Mama out there, I see you and love you. To my village, thank you for showing up and loving me in all my imperfection. To my Hubs, thank you for putting up with my wild visions and helping me stretch through the growing pains of both business and life. To my boys, thank you for being my mirror and showing me both the good and the ugly, I am so grateful for your lessons and unconditional love. To my parents, for giving me life in more ways than just the physical.

Sabrina Greer

Sabrina is a 2x best-selling author and the mastermind behind this popular motherhood guidebook series, which has been coined "*Chicken Soup for the Mama Soul*" by numerous publications. She is the founder of YGTMAMA Inc., a company built on love and focused on inclusive resources and opportunities for mothers. Sabrina also curates a popular collective blog space and is the host of *You've Got This, Mama – The Podcast*.

Sabrina is an aspiring philanthropist who knew from a young age that there was no box for her to comfortably fit into and that her life needed be one by design. After ten years of travelling, modeling, and volunteering overseas, she found home base back in Ontario, Canada where she was born and decided to earn her degree in education and developmental psychology to accredit her world-changing efforts. It did not take long for her to realize that her superpowers lay in entrepreneurship and coaching others to discover their potential. She is a certified NLP/CBT practitioner and life coach. She is the Eastern Canada Ambassador for *Mamas for Mamas*, an award-winning charity that supports mothers in crisis and provides ongoing support to low-income mamas and their kids. Their mission is a future in which no mama or child is left behind.

When she is not writing or attempting to save the world, you will likely find her exploring her wild feminine in nature, near water or momming hard to her three awesome boys; Oliver (13), Sterling (4) and Walker (2).

www.ygtmama.com | www.mamasformamas.ca
ig: @ygtmama | @sabrina.greer.xo
fb: You've Got This, Mama (@ygtmama) | Sabrina Greer

GOLDEN BRICK ROAD
PUBLISHING HOUSE

Locking arms and helping each other down their Golden Brick Road

At Golden Brick Road Publishing House, we lock arms with ambitious people and create success through a collaborative, supportive, and accountable environment. We are a boutique shop that caters to all stages of business around a book. We encourage women empowerment, and gender and cultural equality by publishing single author works from around the world, and creating in-house collaborative author projects for emerging and seasoned authors to join.

Our authors have a safe space to grow and diversify themselves within the genres of poetry, health, sociology, women's studies, business, and personal development. We help those who are natural born leaders, step out and shine! Even if they do not yet fully see it for themselves. We believe in empowering each individual who will then go and inspire an entire community. Our Director, Ky-Lee Hanson, calls this: The Inspiration Trickle Effect.

If you want to be a public figure that is focused on helping people and providing value, but you do not want to embark on the journey alone, then we are the community for you.

To inquire about our collaborative writing opportunities or to bring your own idea into fruition, reach out to us at:

www.goldenbrickroad.pub

Society

Connect with our authors and readers at GBRSociety.com